Narratives of Colonial America
1704-1765

The Lakeside Classics

# NARRATIVES
# OF COLONIAL AMERICA

## 1704-1765

EDITED BY

HOWARD H. PECKHAM

The Lakeside Press

R.R. DONNELLEY & SONS COMPANY

CHICAGO

*Christmas,* 1971

# PUBLISHERS' PREFACE

"NARRATIVES of Colonial America," the 69th in *The Lakeside Classics* series, includes eight personal narratives of pre-Revolutionary life in America. As such, it represents a slight departure from our usual custom of presenting a single first-person story by a single author. Only slight, however, because we have, in fact, confined ourselves to one subject, and that is a cross-section of Colonial life during the decades immediately preceding the Revolutionary War.

The authors range from the enterprising Madam Knight, a Boston business woman, to Major Robert Rogers, who, with his storied Rangers, was a hero of the French and Indian Wars. The book concludes with Lord Adam Gordon's descriptions of Colonial cities as seen through the eyes of a visiting Scotsman. His original manuscript is preserved in The British Museum.

These authentic narratives were gathered for this volume by its editor, Howard H. Peckham, who ferreted them out from many sources. Professor Peckham is director of the renowned William L. Clements Library of the University of Michigan and a professor of history at that same institution. He is an impressive author, editor, and student of American history. Among his books are several Revolutionary War histories, accounts of Indian activities, and Colonial narratives. He has served as editor of a number of manuscript collections as well as periodicals such as Indiana Historical Bulletins and American Heritage.

The Clements Library, which he directs, is one of the country's truly great institutions in the field of American history. Its period of specialization covers the years from 1492 to the middle of the nineteenth century, and its collections consist exclusively of source materials—books, manuscripts, maps, broadsides, newspapers and other documents written or published at the time of the events which they portray.

Professor Peckham is eminently qualified for the job which we asked him to do: select and edit a group of personal narratives which would give an authentic picture of Colonial life and at the same time entertain readers of *The Lakeside Classics*. He has done his job well. We agree with his cogent appraisal of the stories in his Historical Introduction where he says, "This Anthology is designed to be read and enjoyed by persons without a historian's background in early American history, *although this will not be true when they are finished with the book.*" The italics are ours.

Just as we feel most fortunate to have an editor of the caliber of Professor Peckham, we also are pleased to have obtained the services of Robert Williams to research and draw for us the seven maps which accurately and beautifully augment the stories included here. Mr. Williams is an artist and calligrapher whose work is widely esteemed in the academic world.

*The Lakeside Classics* have been printed by the letterpress process since their inception in 1903. Letterpress is defined as printing from a raised surface. It was the common means for printing books at that time, and so was naturally used for the Classics. Even to this day it is an excellent process, and many qualified experts feel that it is the best process by which to print type. However, an ever-increasing share of book printing is being done by offset lithography. This process employs a flat plate with an ink receptive printing image and water receptive non-printing area. After alternate applications of water and ink, the ink is transferred to a rubber blanket which in turn offsets it to the paper, hence the term offset lithography. It has advantages of economy, and over the years we have developed techniques to attain and maintain high quality of the printed image. By changing to this process, we are following the tradition of the founder of *The Lakeside Classics*, Thomas E. Donnelley. He believed that these volumes should demonstrate current methods of book manufacturing, done with special concern for quality in materials and workmanship. This process is the fastest growing segment of our industry, and is also used for other products such as magazines, catalogs, and directories. We produce many of these on large presses feeding from rolls of paper, in one or more colors, and of highest quality.

This Publishers' Preface again gives us an opportunity to comment on our Company for the benefit of those friends who may be interested.

The picture of our operations in 1970 continued with little change into 1971. Both sales and profits continued to grow modestly, in part unfortunately due to inflation. In some areas the demand for our services was relatively soft, while in others it varied from fair to very good at different periods of the year. We were most fortunate in receiving increased orders from some of our customers, and also acquiring some very valuable new accounts.

A very great disappointment was the decision of the publishers of *Look* magazine to discontinue that excellent publication. They faced a discouraging outlook for future advertising sales and increased costs, mainly postage charges.

Throughout the Company, there have been notable gains in efficiency and quality, especially in our newer divisions which are now making positive contributions to overall results. These employ the latest technology to meet the changing needs of our customers.

To the extent that we could have filled a significant amount of idle capacity, 1971 could have been even a better year for the Company.

We are so confident of the long-range prospects

for our Company, that we have embarked on the largest capital investment program in our history. These new projects, of course, will not be fully productive for several years.

On a site we have owned for years in Lancaster, Pennsylvania, a new specialized plant for the production of telephone directories is in the process of construction. This is to fulfill a long-term contract awarded us earlier this year.

Other capital expenditures will be for additional equipment and space at some of our existing locations. These are designed to meet well identified needs in our markets. The remaining expenditures will be to improve existing facilities, using advanced technology to increase productivity and quality.

These, with the unused capacity mentioned above, put us in an excellent position to take advantage of the opportunities and challenges of the future. We are confident the economy will improve, and with it the demand for printing and related services.

Technology is changing in the graphic arts industry as in others. Our operations range in sophistication from computer cathode ray composition which sets type on film from a magnetic tape at 1,000 characters per second to graphic conservation where valuable books and manuscripts are restored or bound by methods essentially unchanged since the Middle Ages. Productivity is hardly comparable but quality is, and quality is a most important objective in all our efforts, including automated controls and material handling. A large press or computer is a tool just as is the simple awl used by the hand binder. The key element in attaining productivity and quality is the skill and dedication of the man or woman using those tools. The skills may change as the tools change. We are most fortunate to have thousands of associates with high skills and great dedication, who can and have adapted to changing and ever more sophisticated technology. They have enabled the Company to prosper and grow by providing a reliable service of quality in response to the changing needs of our customers.

To all our friends within the Company and without, whose interest, help, and support have meant so much to us, warmest thanks and best wishes for the season.

THE PUBLISHERS

Christmas, 1971

# CONTENTS

# ILLUSTRATIONS

# HISTORICAL INTRODUCTION

THIS volume affords a picture of colonial America in the eighteenth century from a selection of personal narratives. Our hope was to present a cross-section of that life, but this was impossible: at the elite end of the spectrum many important people did not keep diaries or leave memoirs, while at the populous end many people could not or did not write. In addition, dull diaries were discarded, and some famous accounts are too recently available in other reprint forms. Yet within these restrictions eight narratives—personal, varied, interesting—balanced between civil and military adventures—were found. Within the covers are recurrent themes of peace and war, security and danger, hope and disappointment, freedom and restriction, not unlike the present century.

We begin with a travel narrative of 1704–05 by an indomitable woman and then move southwestward to a descriptive account of French life in New Orleans in 1743. In contrast is the life of an Indian captive in Ohio in the years 1755 to 1760. This period saw the turbulence of the French and Indian War, and two actions are described: an American chaplain writes of the disastrous English attack on Fort Ticonderoga in 1758, and the commander of Rogers' Rangers himself tells of his remarkable raid on St. Francis the next year.

An American-born lieutenant details what it was like to be shut up in Fort Detroit during Chief Pontiac's siege in 1763. Another woman writer recalls the pleasant life of the Anglo-Dutch children in Albany in the 1760's, while a British aristocrat traveled the length of the Atlantic seaboard in 1765 and seemed to fall in love with our growing towns. There you have a sampler of the variety of life here in the seven decades before the American Revolution began.

Even these few narratives indicate the astonishing variety of life and environment in America. In peace and in war a new society was emerging. It was already assuming a revolutionary tone in the sense of appealing to the discontented of Europe while at the same time inspiring American colonials with new hopes and aspirations.

The introductions to the several pieces provide, I trust, the setting necessary to understand and enjoy them. A few footnotes identify certain persons or places and explain allusions. Occasional irrelevant or tedious details are omitted. Above all, every effort was made to render these early and some-times private narratives clear on first reading. Hence, cryptic abbreviations have been spelled out; punctuation, capitalization, and spelling have been modernized; occasional rambling sentences have been broken up—all in an attempt to save the reader from going over the same lines several times in order to extract the meaning. This anthology is designed to be read and enjoyed by persons without a historian's background in early American history, although this will not be true when they are finished with the book.

I am indebted to the Library of Congress, the Fort Ticonderoga Museum Library, the Massachusetts Historical Society, the State Historian of New York, and to my own William L. Clements Library for information, illustrations, and permissions.

HOWARD H. PECKHAM

University of Michigan
Ann Arbor, Michigan, 1971

Narratives of Colonial America
1704-1765

# 1

## Madam Knight's Journal

*

### *A Woman Travels to New York*
### 1704

# A Woman Travels to New York
## 1704

*Born at Boston in 1666, Sarah Kemble was the daughter of a merchant. When he died in 1689, she was already married to Captain Richard Knight, a shipmaster and a widower much older than herself. He was gone for extended periods, and Sarah found it necessary to pursue some remunerative occupation to support herself, her mother, and her small daughter. Business, however, was entirely congenial to her.*

*She kept some sort of a shop in her parent's house near the North Square, she apparently took in roomers and boarders, she drafted legal documents, copied court records, and eventually she acted as administrator of estates. Obviously she was not only intelligent and educated, but ambitious and enterprising as well. Later on she opened a school to teach writing. In true American style she prospered through hard work.*

*One member of her household was a young widow who in July 1704 was married to Sarah Knight's well-to-do cousin, Caleb Trowbridge of New Haven, Connecticut. A few weeks later the bride was a widow again. Apparently in the interest* of settling that estate, Madam Knight, as she was called, started for New Haven on October 2 to confer with Thomas Trowbridge, the father of the deceased groom. The trip on horseback by herself was a serious undertaking, and for a woman to go alone was extraordinary to say the least.

Her route from Boston was south through Dedham down to Providence, although she did not enter the town, then around Narragansett Bay to Kingston, Rhode Island. Turning west she entered Connecticut through Stonington, passed through New London, Killingworth, and Saybrook, reaching New Haven on October 7. There she visited her kinsman and transacted business for two months. Her mission still uncompleted and waiting upon "some concerns in New York," Mr. Trowbridge prepared to go there on her behalf, and Madam Knight decided to accompany him.

The journey resumed on December 6, with the travelers touching at Fairfield and Norwalk, then Rye and New Rochelle in New York before reaching the city in three days. A few days before Christmas (not observed in Puritan New England), the return journey was made to New Haven. Continued delays aroused Madam Knight's suspicion that no settlement was intended, but by her patience and resolution "we came to an accommodation and distribution" of the estate. It was now February 1705, *in the dead of winter, before she began making her way back to Boston, which she reached on March 3.*

*Madam's life may be quickly concluded. Her husband, if living when she made this journey, was abroad and died soon afterward. Her mother died in 1712. The next year her 24-year-old daughter Elizabeth married Col. John Livingston of New London. Madam Knight then sold her Boston house and moved to New London, where she owned several farms, speculated in land, kept a shop and a tavern and died in 1727 leaving a large estate.*

*During her trip of 1704–05 she kept a daily diary and wrote this account from her notes. It remained in her daughter's possession until it passed to a relative who administered her estate. Theodore Dwight of New York secured a copy and first published it in 1825. Subsequently the original manuscript—or the copy he saw—disappeared. The journal was reprinted in a Boston weekly, then in a magazine, still without explanatory notes. Four separate reprints have appeared, all of them limited editions, the last in 1935; only the 1865 edition has notes. It remains a delightful report.*

*When she made her trip, Madam Knight was a God-fearing woman of 38, but hardly pious. She was not so concerned for the state of her soul as for the comfort of her body. Little of people she met escaped her notice, and these penetrating details* give her journal its charming realism. It opens a window for us on domestic life and manners in early New England and reveals by contrast the life in New York. The crudeness of some habitations is lessened by warm hospitality, frightening nighttime rides alternate with pleasant daylight trots, good meals balance off some appalling dishes, and beds vary then as they do today. Through her we meet some interesting persons at work and at play. As for the author's self-revelation, she was clearly possessed of courage, humor, a shrewd eye, and a cheerful accommodation to life and its discomforts. She charmed her hosts in New Haven and New York and quickly made their friends her friends. She emerges as an extremely likeable person, and we are glad that she prospered. Her circumstances might have overwhelmed a less resolute and energetic person.

Inasmuch as there is no original manuscript to follow, and as Mr. Dwight admitted to making some changes and omissions, this editor has not hesitated to render the journal as readable as possible today by correcting her original spelling and punctuation, reducing her excessive capitalization, extending some abbreviations, and occasionally straightening out her confused syntax, all in an effort to save the reader from going over the lines twice to obtain their meaning. Her poetical effusions

and two irrelevant anecdotes she was told have
been omitted.

The reader is referred to the map to follow
Madam Knight's route and the towns she names.
No effort has been made to elaborate on everyone
she met, and she identifies some of them adequately.
The journal begins with her departure.

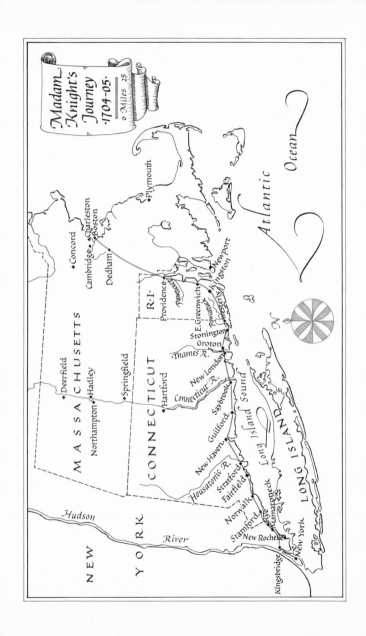

Madam Knight's Journey ·1704-05·

0  Miles  25

Atlantic Ocean

Plymouth

Concord  Charleston
Cambridge·  Boston
Dedham·

R.I.
Pawtucket
Providence·  E. Greenwich  Newport
Pawcatuck  Kingston
Westerly
Stonington
Groton
Thames R.
New London

Deerfield·
Hadley·  Springfield·
Northampton·  Hartford·
Connecticut R.
Saybrook

MASSACHUSETTS

CONNECTICUT

Guilford

New Haven·
Housatonic R.  Stratford·
Fairfield·
Norwalk·
Stamford·  Mamaroneck
New Rochelle·  Rye
Kingsbridge·  New York

Long Island Sound

LONG ISLAND

Hudson

NEW  YORK  River

# Her Journal

MONDAY, *October the second, 1704*. About three o'clock [in the] afternoon I began my journey from Boston to New Haven, being about two hundred miles. My kinsman, Capt. Robert Luist, waited on me as far as Dedham, where I was to meet the western post.[1]

I visited the Reverend Mr. Belcher, the minister of the town, and tarried there till evening, in hopes the post would come along. But he not coming, I resolved to go to Billings's where he used to lodge, being 12 miles farther. But being ignorant of the way, Madam Billings,[2] seeing no persuasions of her good spouse's or hers could prevail with me to lodge there that night, very kindly went with me to the tavern, where I hoped to get my guide, and desired the hostess to inquire of her guests whether any of them would go with me. But they being tied by the lips to a pewter engine,[3] scarcely allowed themselves

[1] Luist was a shopkeeper in Charlestown. The western post was a mail carrier who rode alternately to Hartford and Saybrook, Conn., and there exchanged letters with a rider from New York. Saybrook is now Old Saybrook and also the location of one of the R. R. Donnelley plants.

[2] Obviously a slip of the pen: she means Mrs. Belcher, wife of the Rev. Joseph Belcher, pastor of the church in Dedham.

[3] A humorous reference to pewter mugs of ale which seemed to move under their own power from table top to mouth.

time to say what clownish . . . [*Here half a page of the manuscript is gone.*] . . . pieces of eight, I told her no, I would not be accessory to such extortion.

"Then John shan't go," says she. "No, indeed, shan't he;" and held forth at that rate a long time, that I began to fear I was got among the quaking tribe, believing not a limber-tongued sister among them could outdo Madam Hostess.

Upon this, to my no small surprise, son John arose and gravely demanded what I would give him to go with me?

"Give you," says I, "are you John?"

"Yes," says he, "for want of a better;" and behold! this John looked as old as my host and perhaps had been a man in the last century.

"Well, Mr. John," says I, "make your demands."

"Why, half a piece of eight and a dram,"[4] says John.

I agreed and gave him a dram (now) in hand to bind the bargain. My hostess catechized John for going so cheap, saying his poor wife would break her heart . . . [*Here another half page of the manuscript is gone.*] His shape on his horse resembled a globe on a gate post. His habit, horse, and furniture, its looks and goings, incomparably answered the rest.

Thus jogging on with an easy pace, my guide telling me it was dangerous to ride hard in the night (which his horse had the sense to avoid), he

[4]Pieces of eight were the Spanish dollar. A dram was a small drink of liquor.

entertained me with the adventures he had passed by late riding, and eminent dangers he had escaped, so that, remembering the heroes in *Parismus* and the *Knight of the Oracle*,[5] I didn't know but I had met with a prince disguised.

When we had ridden about an hour, we came into a thick swamp, which by reason of a great fog very much startled me, it being now very dark. But nothing dismayed John; he had encountered a thousand and a thousand such swamps, having a universal knowledge in the woods, and readily answered all my inquiries, which were not a few.

In about an hour, or something more, after we left the swamp, we came to Billings's, where I was to lodge. My guide dismounted and very complaisantly helped me down and showed [me] the door, signing to me with his hand to go in, which I gladly did—but had not gone many steps into the room ere I was interrogated by a young lady I understood afterwards was the eldest daughter of the family with these, or words to this purpose (viz.).

"Law for me, what in the world brings you here at this time a night? I never see a woman on the road so dreadful late, in all the days of my 'versall[6] life.

[5] An allusion to two English romances by Emanual Ford: *Parismus, the Renowned Prince of Bohemia* (London, 1598) and *The Famous History of Montelion, Knight of the Oracle* (London, *c.* 1630). Both were popular and were reprinted many times in the next century.

[6] Usually spelled versal and an abbreviation for universal; used here to refer to a single or one life.

Who are you? Where are you going? I'm scared out of my wits"—with much now of the same kind.

I stood aghast, preparing to reply, when in came my guide. To him Madam turned, roaring out: "Lawful heart, John, is it you? How de do! Where in the world are you going with this woman? Who is she?"

John made no answer, but sat down in the corner, fumbled out his black junk[7] and saluted that instead of Deb. She then turned again to me and fell anew into her silly questions, without asking me to sit down.

I told her she treated me very rudely, and I did not think it my duty to answer her unmannerly questions. But to get rid of them, I told her I came there to have the post's company with me tomorrow on my journey, &c. Miss stared awhile, drew a chair, bid me sit, and then ran upstairs and put on two or three rings (or else I had not seen them before) and returning, set herself just before me, showing the way to Reding, that I might see her ornaments, perhaps to gain the more respect. But her Gran'am's new rung sow, had it appeared would [have] affected me as much. I paid honest John with money and dram according to contract and dismissed him, and prayed Miss to show me where I must lodge. She conducted me to a parlor in a little back leanto, which was almost filled with the bedstead, which was so high that I was forced to climb on a chair to get up to the wretched bed that lay on

[7] Junk was a tobacco pipe.

it; on which having stretched my tired limbs and laid my head on a sad-colored pillow, I began to think on the transactions of the past day.

*Tuesday, October the third,* about 8 in the morning, I with the post proceeded forward without observing anything remarkable; and about two [in the] afternoon, arrived at the post's second stage, where the western post met him and exchanged letters. Here, having called for something to eat, the woman brought in a twisted thing like a cable, but something whiter, and laying it on the board tugged for life to bring it into a capacity to spread; which having with great pains accomplished, she served in a dish of pork and cabbage, I suppose the remains of dinner. The sauce was of a deep purple, which I thought was boiled in her dye kettle; the bread was Indian,[8] and every thing on the table service agreeable to these. I, being hungry, got a little down; but my stomach was soon cloyed, and what cabbage I swallowed served me for a cud the whole day after.

Having here discharged the ordinary[9] for self and guide (as I understood was the custom) about three [in the] afternoon [I] went on with my third guide, who rode very hard; and having crossed Providence ferry, we came to a river which they generally ride through.[10] But I dare not venture, so the post got a

---

[8] That is, made with maize: corn bread.
[9] A tavern or inn where meals were served.
[10] Pawtuxet River.

lad and canoe to carry me to tother side, and he rode through and led my horse. The canoe was very small and shallow, so that when we were in she seemed ready to take in water, which greatly terrified me and caused me to be very circumspect, sitting with my hands fast on each side, my eyes steady, not daring so much as to lodge my tongue a hair's breadth more on one side of my mouth than tother, nor so much as think on Lot's wife, for a wry thought would have overset our wherry;[11] but was soon put out of this pain by feeling the canoe on shore, which I soon almost saluted with my feet; and rewarded my sculler, again mounted and made the best of our way forward.

The road here was very even and the day pleasant, it being now near sunset. But the post told me we had near 14 miles to ride to the next stage (where we were to lodge). I asked him of the rest of the road, foreseeing we must travel in the night. He told me there was a bad river we were to ride through which was so very fierce a horse could sometimes hardly stem it; but it was but narrow, and we should soon be over. I cannot express the concern of mind this relation set me in: no thoughts but those of the dangerous river could entertain my imagination, and they were as formidable as various, still tormenting me with blackest ideas of my approaching fate—sometimes seeing myself drowning, otherwhiles drowned, and at the best like a holy

[11] A long light canoe.

sister just come out of a spiritual bath in dripping garments.

Now was the glorious luminary, with his swift coursers, arrived at his stage, leaving poor me with the rest of this part of the lower world in darkness, with which we were soon surrounded. The only glimmering we now had was from the spangled skies, whose imperfect reflections rendered every object formidable. Each lifeless trunk, with its shattered limbs, appeared an armed enemy; and every little stump like a ravenous devourer. Nor could I so much as discern my guide when at any distance, which added to the terror.

Thus absolutely lost in thought and dying with the very thoughts of drowning, I came up with the post, which I did not see till even with his horse. He told me he stopped for me, and we rode on very deliberately a few paces when we entered a thicket of trees and shrubs, and I perceived by the horse's going we were on the descent of a hill, which as we came nearer the bottom 'twas totally dark with the trees that surrounded it. But I knew by the going of the horse we had entered the water, which my guide told me was the hazardous river he had told me of; and he, riding up close to my side, bid me not fear —we should be over immediately.[12] I now rallied all the courage I was mistress of, knowing that I must either venture my fate of drowning, or be left like

[12] Probably the Mascachuge River, south of East Greenwich.

the children in the wood. So as the post bid me, I gave reins to my nag, and sitting as steady as just before in the canoe, in a few minutes got safe to the other side, which he told me was the Narragansett country.

Here we found great difficulty in traveling, the way being very narrow and on each side the trees and bushes gave us very unpleasant welcomes with their branches and boughs, which we could not avoid, it being so exceeding dark. My guide, as before so now, put on harder than I with my weary bones could follow, so left me and the way behind him. Now returned my distressed apprehensions of the place where I was: the dolesome woods, my company next to none, going I knew not whither, and encompassed with terrifying darkness, the least of which was enough to startle a more masculine courage. Added to which [were] the reflections, as in the afternoon of the day, that my call was very questionable, which till then I had not so prudently as I ought considered.

Now coming to the foot of a hill I found great difficulty in ascending, but being got to the top was there amply recompensed with the friendly appearance of the kind conductress of the night, just then advancing above the horizontal line. The raptures which the sight of that fair planet produced in me caused me for the moment to forget my present weariness and past toils; and inspired me for most the remaining way with very diverting thoughts, some of which with the other occurrences of the day, I reserved to note down when I should come to my stage. . .

From hence we kept on, with more ease than before, the way being smooth and even, the night warm and serene, and the tall and thick trees at a distance, especially when the moon glared light through the branches, filled my imagination with the pleasant delusion of a sumptuous city, filled with famous buildings and churches, with their spiring steeples, balconies, galleries, and I know not what: grandeurs which I had heard of and which the stories of foreign countries had given me the idea of. . .

Being thus agreeably entertained without a thought of any thing but thoughts themselves, I on a sudden was roused from these pleasing imaginations by the post's sounding his horn, which assured me he was arrived at the stage where we were to lodge, and that music was then most musical and agreeable to me.

Being come to Mr. Havens', I was very civilly received and courteously entertained in a clean comfortable house;[13] and the good woman was very active in helping off my riding clothes and then asked what I would eat. I told her I had some chocolate, if she would prepare it; which with the help of some milk and a little clean brass kettle she soon effected to my satisfaction. I then betook me

[13] Haven's tavern was in North Kingston.

to my apartment, which was a little room parted
from the kitchen by a single board partition; where,
after I had noted the occurrences of the past day, I
went to bed, which though pretty hard yet neat and
handsome.

But I could get no sleep, because of the clamor of
some of the town topers in next room, who were
entered into a strong debate concerning the signifi-
cation of the name of their country, (viz.) *Narragansett.* One said it was named so by the Indians,
because there grew a briar there of a prodigious
height and bigness, the like hardly ever known,
called by the Indians Narragansett; and quoted an
Indian of so barbarous a name for his author that
I could not write it. His antagonist replied no—it
was from a spring it had its name, which he well
knew where it was, which was extreme cold in summer and as hot as could be imagined in the winter,
which was much resorted to by the natives and by
them called Narragansett (hot and cold), and that
was the original of their place's name—with a thousand impertinances not worth notice which he
uttered with such a roaring voice and thundering
blows with the fist of wickedness on the table that it
pierced my very head. I heartily fretted and wished
'em tongue tied; but with as little success as a friend
of mine once who was (as she said) kept a whole
night awake on a journey by a country lieutenant
and a sergeant, ensign and a deacon contriving how
to bring a triangle into a square. They kept calling

for tother gill, which while they were swallowing, was some intermission; but presently like oil to fire increased the flame . . .

*Wednesday, October 4th.* About four in the morning we set out for Kingston (for so was the town called) with a French doctor in our company. He and the post put on very furiously, so that I could not keep up with them, only as now and then they'd stop till they see me. This road was poorly furnished with accommodations for travelers, so that we were forced to ride 22 miles by the post's account, but nearer thirty by mine, before we could bait[14] so much as our horses, which I exceedingly complained of. But the post encouraged me by saying we should be well accommodated anon at Mr. Devill's, a few miles farther.[15] But I questioned whether we ought to go to the Devil to be helped out of affliction.

However, like the rest of deluded souls that post to the infernal den, we made all possible speed to this Devill's habitation, where alighting in full assurance of good accommodation, we were going in. But meeting his two daughters, as I supposed twins they so nearly resembled each other, both in features and habit, and looked as old as the Devil himself and quite as ugly, we desired entertainment, but could hardly get a word out of 'em till with

[14] To stop for food and drink.
[15] Probably Mr. Davell in Westerly, but then spelled Devill. Madam Knight continued to make puns about his name.

our importunity, telling them our necessity, &c.
they called the old sophister,[16] who was as sparing
of his words as his daughters had been, and no, or
none, was the replies he made us to our demands.
He differed only in this from the old fellow in
tother country: he let us depart . . .

Thus leaving this habitation of cruelty, we went
forward; and arriving at an ordinary about two
miles farther, found tolerable accommodation. But
our hostess, being a pretty full mouthed old creature,
entertained our fellow traveler, the French doctor,
with innumerable complaints of her bodily infirmi-
ties; and whispered to him so loud that all the house
had as full a hearing as he, which was very diverting to
the company (of which there was a great many) as one
might see by their sneering. But poor weary I slipped
out to enter my mind in my journal and left my great
landlady with her talkative guests to themselves.

From hence we proceeded (about ten, forenoon)
through the Narragansett country pretty leisurely;
and about one [in the] afternoon came to Paukataug
River[17] which was about two hundred paces over
and now very high, and no way over to tother side
but this. I dared not venture to ride through, my
courage at best in such cases but small, and now at
the lowest ebb by reason of my weary, very weary,

[16] A thinker or philosopher, with a trace of specious rea-
soning. Madam Knight is being facetious about her host.
[17] The Pawcatuck River forms part of the lower boundary
between Rhode Island and Connecticut.

hungry and uneasy circumstances. So taking leave of my company, though with no little reluctance that I could not proceed with them on my journey, stopped at a little cottage just by the river to wait the water's falling, which the old man that lived there said would be in a little time, and he would conduct me safe over.

This little hut was one of the wretchedest I ever saw [for] a habitation for human creatures. It was supported with shores enclosed with clapboards laid on lengthwise, and so much asunder that the light came through everywhere; the door tied on with a cord in the place of hinges; the floor the bare earth; no windows but such as the thin covering afforded, nor any furniture but a bed with a glass bottle hanging at the head on it; an earthen cup, a small pewter basin, a board with sticks to stand on instead of a table, and a block or two in the corner instead of chairs. The family were the old man, his wife and two children, all and every part being the picture of poverty. Notwithstanding, both the hut and its inhabitants were very clean and tidy: to the crossing [of] the old proverb that bare walls make giddy housewives.

I blessed myself that I was not one of this miserable crew . . . I had scarce done thinking when an Indian-like animal came to the door, on a creature very much like himself in mien and feature, as well as ragged clothing; and having lit makes an awkward scratch with his Indian shoe and a nod, sits on the

block, fumbles out his black junk, dips it in the
ashes, and presents it piping hot to his muschee-
to's[18] and fell to sucking like a calf without speaking
for near a quarter of an hour. At length the old man
said, "How does Sarah do?" who I understood was
the wretch's wife, and daughter to the old man.

He replied, "As well as can be expected" &c. So
I remembered the old saw and supposed I knew
Sarah's case.

But he being, as I understood, going over the river,
as ugly as he was I was glad to ask him to show me
the way to Saxton's at Stonington; which he prom-
ising, I ventured over with the old man's assistance;
who having rewarded to content, with my tatter-
tailed guide I rode on very slowly through Stonington, where the road was very stony and uneven. I
asked the fellow as we went diverse questions of
the place and way, &c. I being arrived at my
country [man Joseph] Saxton's at Stonington, was
very well accommodated both as to victuals and
lodging, the only good of both I had found since
my setting out.

Here I heard there was an old man and his
daughter to come that way bound to New London;
and being now destitute of a guide, gladly waited
for them, being in so good a harbor, and accordingly
Thursday, October the 5th, about 3 in the afternoon,

---

[18] A foreign word, misspelled and unclear. Obviously she
means his lips, but she may have been trying to indicate that
he placed the pipe stem between his mustache and beard.

I set forward with neighbor Polly and Jemima, a girl about 18 years old, who he said he had been to fetch out of the Narragansetts, and said they had rode thirty miles that day on a sorry lean jade,[19] with only a bag under her for a pillion, which the poor girl often complained was very uneasy.

We made good speed along, which made poor Jemima make many a sour face, the mare being a very hard trotter; and after many a hearty and bitter "Oh," she at length lowed out: "Lawful heart, father! This bare mare hurts me dingly.[20] I'm direful sore, I vow;" with many words to that purpose.

"Poor child," says gaffer, "she used to serve your mother so."

"I don't care how mother used to do," quoth Jemima in a passionate tone. At which the old man laughed and kicked his jade on the side, which made her jolt ten times harder.

About seven that evening we came to New London ferry. Here by reason of a very high wind we met with great difficulty in getting over: the boat tossed exceedingly, and our horses capered at a very surprising rate and set us all in a fright; especially poor Jemima, who desired her father to say so-jack[21]

---

[19] A mean, vicious or playful horse, who probably had seen better days.

[20] Apparently an attempt to make an adverb out of "dingle," meaning "to tingle."

[21] Here "so" is used in its meaning of "that will do!" a word sometimes used to quiet animals, as in "So boss" to a cow, or "So jack" to a mule.

to the jade to make her stand. But the careless parent, taking no notice of her repeated desires, she roared out in a passionate manner:

"Pray sooth, father, are you deaf? Say so-jack to the jade, I tell you."

The dutiful parent obeyed, saying so-jack, so-jack as gravely as if he'd been to saying catechism after young miss, who with her fright looked of all colors in the rainbow.

Being safely arrived at the house of Mrs. Prentice[22] in New London, I treated neighbor Polly and daughter for their diverting company and bid them farewell; and between nine and ten at night waited on the Rev. Mr. Gurdon Saltonstall,[23] minister of the town, who kindly invited me to stay that night at his house, where I was very handsomely and plentifully treated and lodged; and made good the great character I had before heard concerning him: viz. that he was the most affable, courteous, generous and best of men.

*Friday, October 6th.* I got up very early, in order to hire somebody to go with me to New Haven, being in great perplexity at the thoughts of proceeding alone, which my most hospitable entertainer ob-

---

[22] Mrs. Prentis, a widow, kept a tavern on Main Street, next door to the Rev. Mr. Saltonstall.

[23] Gurdon Saltonstall (1666–1724) was born in Massachusetts, graduated from Harvard, and became minister at New London in 1691. He was adviser to Gov. Fitz-John Winthrop, on whose death in 1707 the Assembly asked him to assume the governorship. He was re-elected annually until his death.

serving, himself went and soon returned with a young gentleman of the town whom he could confide in to go with me; and about eight this morning with Mr. Joshua Wheeler, my new guide, taking leave of this worthy gentleman, we advanced on towards Saybrook.

The roads all along this way are very bad, encumbered with rocks and mountainous passages which were very disagreeable to my tired carcass; but we went on with a moderate pace which made the journey more pleasant. But after about eight miles riding in going over a bridge under which the river ran very swift, my horse stumbled and very narrowly escaped falling over into the water, which extremely frightened me. But through God's goodness I met with no harm, and mounting again in about half a mile's riding came to an ordinary, were well entertained by a woman of about seventy and vantage, but of as sound intellect as one of seventeen. She entertained Mr. Wheeler with some passages of a wedding awhile ago at a place hard by, the bridegroom being about her age or something above, saying his children was dreadfully against their father's marrying, which she condemned them extremely for.

From hence we went pretty briskly forward and arrived at Saybrook ferry about two of the clock, afternoon; and crossing it we called at an inn to bait (foreseeing we should not have such another opportunity till we came to Killingworth). Landlady came in, with her hair about her ears and hands at full pay scratching. She told us she had some mutton which she would broil, which I was glad to hear; but I suppose forgot to wash her scratchers. In a little time she brought it in, but it being pickled, and my guide said it smelled strong of head sauce, we left it and paid sixpence apiece for our dinners, which was only smell.

So we put forward with all speed and about seven at night came to Killingworth, and were tolerably well with travelers' fare and lodged there that night.

*Saturday, October 7th*, we set out early in the morning and being something unacquainted with the way, having asked it of some we met, they told us we must ride a mile or two and turn down a lane on the right hand; and by their direction we rode on but not yet coming to the turning, we met a young fellow and asked him how far it was to the lane which turned down towards Guilford. He said we must ride a little farther and turn down by the corner of Uncle Sam's lot. My guide vented his spleen at the lubber;[24] and we soon after came into the road and keeping still on, without anything further remarkable, about two o'clock, afternoon, we arrived at New Haven, where I was received with all possible respect and civility. Here I discharged Mr. Wheeler with a reward to his satisfaction and took some time to rest after so long and toilsome a journey; and informed myself of the manners and

[24] A lout, or clumsy, stupid person.

customs of the place, and at the same time employed myself in the affair I went there upon.

They are governed by the same laws as we in Boston (or little differing) throughout this whole colony of Connecticut. And much the same way of church government, and many of them good, sociable people, and I hope religious too; but a little too much independent in their principles and, as I have been told, were formerly in their zeal very rigid in their administrations towards such as their laws made offenders, even to a harmless kiss or innocent merriment among young people: whipping being a frequent and counted an easy punishment, about which as other crimes the judges were absolute in their sentences . . .

Their diversions in this part of the country are on Lecture days and Training days mostly: on the former there is riding from town to town.

And on Training days the youth divert themselves by shooting at the target, as they call it (but it very much resembles a pillory), where he that hits nearest the white has some yards of red ribbon presented him, which being tied to his hatband, the two ends streaming down his back, he is led away in triumph with great applause, as the winners of the Olympic games. They generally marry very young: the males oftener as I am told under twenty than above; they generally make public weddings and have a way something singular [as they say] in some of them, viz. just before joining hands the bridegroom quits the place, who is soon followed by the bridesmen and as it were dragged back to duty—being the reverse to the former practice among us to steal ms. pride.[25]

There are great plenty of oysters all along by the seaside, as far as I rode in the colony, and those very good. And they generally live very well and comfortably in their families; but too indulgent [especially the farmers] to their slaves, suffering too great familiarity from them, permitting them to sit at table and eat with them (as they say to save time).

They told me that there was a farmer lived near the town where I lodged who had some difference with his slave, concerning something the master had promised him and did not punctually perform; which caused some hard words between them. But at length they put the matter to arbitration and bound themselves to stand to the award of such as they named—which done, the arbitrators having heard the allegations of both parties, ordered the master to pay 40 shillings to [the slave] and acknowledge his fault. And so the matter ended: the poor master very honestly standing to the award.

There are everywhere in the towns as I passed a number of Indians, the natives of the country, and are the most savage of all the savages of that kind that I had ever seen, little or no care taken (as I heard upon inquiry) to make them otherwise. They

[25] In the 1858 reprinting these last two words were rendered "ms Bride," probably meaning "Mistress Bride."

have in some places lands of their own, and governed by laws of their own making; they marry many wives and at pleasure put them away and on the least dislike or fickle humor, on either side, saying "Stand away" to one another is a sufficient divorce. And indeed those uncomely "stand aways" are too much in vogue among the English in this indulgent colony, as their records plentifully prove, and that on very trivial matters, of which some have been told me but are not proper to be related by a female pen, though some of that foolish sex have had too large a share in the story.

If the natives commit any crime on their own precincts among themselves, the English take no cognizance of. But if on the English ground, they are punishable by our laws. They mourn for their dead by blacking their faces and cutting their hair after an awkward and frightful manner; but can't bear you should mention the names of their dead relations to them. They trade most for rum, for which they'd hazard their very lives; and the English fit him generally as well by seasoning it plentifully with water.

They gave the title of merchant to every trader, who rate their goods according to the time and specie they pay in: viz. pay, money, pay as money, and trusting. *Pay* is grain, pork, beef, &c. at the prices set by the General Court that year. *Money* is pieces of eight, rials, or Boston or Bay shillings (as they call them) or good hard money, as sometimes

silver coin is termed by them; also wampum, viz.
Indian beads, which serve for change. *Pay as money*
is provisions, as aforesaid one-third cheaper than the
Assembly or General Court sets it. And *Trust* as
they and the merchant agree for time.

Now when the buyer comes to ask for a commodity, sometimes before the merchant answers that
he has it, he says: "Is your pay ready?" Perhaps the
chap replies, "Yes."

"What do you pay in?" says the merchant.

The buyer having answered, then the price is set.
As suppose he wants a sixpenny knife: in pay it is
12 pence; in pay as money eight pence; and hard
money its own price, viz 6 pence. It seems a very intricate way of trade, and what *Lex Mercatoria*[26] had
not thought of.

Being at a merchant's house, in comes a tall country fellow, with his alfogeos[27] full of tobacco, for
they seldom lose their cud, but keep chewing and
spitting as long as their eyes are open. He advanced
to the middle of the room, made an awkward nod,
and spitting a large deal of aromatic tincture, he
gave a scrape with his shovel-like shoe, leaving a
small shovelful of the dirt on the floor, made a full
stop, hugging his own pretty body with his hands
under his arms, stood staring round him like a cat

[26] Literally, law merchant, but more likely mercantile law.
[27] Possibly a misspelling of the Spanish word *alforjas*,
meaning saddlebags. Here it may refer to tobacco pouches,
although she seems to mean his cheeks puffed out with
chewing tobacco.

let out of a basket. At last, like the creature Balaam rode on,[28] he opened his mouth and said: "Have you any ribbons for hatbands to sell, I pray?"

The questions and answers about the pay being passed, the ribbon is brought and opened. Bumpkin Simpers cries: "It's confounded gay, I vow;" and beckoning to the door, in comes Joan Tawdry, dropping about 50 curtsies, and stands by him. He shows her the ribbon.

"Law you," says she, "It's right gent, do you take it. Tis dreadful pretty." Then she inquires, "Have you any hood silk, I pray?" Which being brought and bought, "Have you any thread silk to sew it with?" says she, which being accommodated with, they depart.

They generally stand after they come in a great while speechless, and sometimes don't say a word till they are asked what they want, which I impute to the awe they stand in of the merchants, whom they are constantly almost indebted to; and must take what they bring without liberty to choose for themselves; but they serve them as well by making the merchants stay long enough for their pay.

We may observe here the great necessity and benefit both of education and conversation; for these people have as large a portion of mother wit, and sometimes larger, than those who have been brought up in cities; but for want of improvements render themselves almost ridiculous, as above. I should be

[28] Biblical reference to Balaam's ass.

glad if they would leave such follies and am sure all that love clean houses (at least) would be glad on it too.

They are generally very plain in their dress, throughout all the colony, as I saw, and follow one another in their modes, that you may know where they belong, especially the women, meet them where you will.

Their chief red letter day is St. Election, which is annually observed according to charter, to choose their governor: a blessing they can never be thankful enough for, as they will find if ever it be their hard fortune to lose it. The present governor in Connecticut is the Honorable John Winthrop, Esq., a gentleman of an ancient and honorable family whose father was governor here sometime before, and his grandfather had been governor of the Massachusetts. This gentleman is a very courteous and affable person much given to hospitality, and has by his good services gained the affections of the people as much as any who had been before him in that post.

*December 6th.* Being by this time well recruited and rested after my journey, my business lying unfinished by some concerns at New York depending thereupon, my kinsman, Mr. Thomas Trowbridge of New Haven, must needs take a journey there before it could be accomplished, I resolved to go there in company with him and a man of the town which I engaged to wait on me there. Accordingly, December 6th we set out from New Haven and about

11 same morning came to Stratford ferry, which crossing, about two miles on the other side baited our horses and would have eaten a morsel ourselves, but the pumpkin and Indian-mixed bread had such an aspect, and the bare-legged punch so awkward, or rather awful, a sound, that we left both and proceeded forward, and about seven at night came to Fairfield, where we met with good entertainment and lodged.

And early next morning set forward to Norwalk, from its half Indian name North-walk, when about 12 at noon we arrived and had a dinner of fried venison, very savory. Landlady wanting some pepper in the seasoning, bid the girl hand her the spice in the *gay* cup on the shelf. From hence we hasted towards Rye, walking and leading our horses near a mile together up a prodigious high hill; and so riding till about nine at night and there arrived and took up our lodgings at an ordinary which a French family kept.

Here being very hungry, I desired a fricasee, which the Frenchman undertaking managed so contrary to my notion of cookery that I hastened to bed supperless. And being shown the way up a pair of stairs which had such a narrow passage that I had [been] almost stopped by the bulk of my body, but arriving at my apartment found it to be a little leanto chamber furnished amongst other rubbish with a high bed and a low one, a long table, a bench and a bottomless chair. Little Miss went to scratch up my kennel,[29] which rustled as if she'd been in the barn amongst the husks, and [I] suppose such was the contents of the ticking. Nevertheless, being exceeding weary, down I laid my poor carcass (never more tired) and found my covering as scanty as my bed was hard.

Anon I heard another rustling nose in the room [and] called to know the matter. Little Miss said she was making a bed for the men, who, when they were in bed, complained their legs lay out of it by reason of its shortness. My poor bones complained bitterly, not being used to such lodgings, and so did the man who was with us; and poor I made but one groan, which was from the time I went to bed to the time I rose, which was about three in the morning. Sitting up by the fire till light and having discharged our ordinary, which was as dear as if we had had far better fare, we took our leave of Monsieur and about seven in the morn came to New Rochelle, a French town,[30] where we had a good breakfast. And in the strength of that about an hour before sunset got to York.

Here I applied myself to Mr. Burroughs,[31] a merchant to whom I was recommended by my kinsman, Capt. Prout, and received great civilities from him and his spouse who were now both deaf but

[29] A deprecatory remark comparing her accommodations to an animal's den.

[30] New Rochelle was a relatively new town, settled in 1688 by French Huguenots.

[31] Probably Thomas Burroughs, a prominent merchant.

very agreeable in their conversation, diverting me with pleasant stories of their knowledge in Britain, from whence they both came. . .

Mr. Burroughs went with me to vendue[32] where I bought about 100 reams of paper which was retaken in a flyboat from Holland and sold very reasonably here — some ten, some eight shillings per ream by the lot, which was ten reams in a lot. And at the vendue I made a great many acquaintances amongst the good women of the town who courteously invited me to their houses and generously entertained me.

The city of New York is a pleasant, well compacted place situated on a commodious river which is a fine harbor for shipping.[33] The buildings [are] brick generally, very stately and high, though not altogether like ours in Boston. The bricks in some of the houses are of diverse colors and laid in checkers; being glazed, look very agreeable. The insides of them are neat to admiration, the wooden work, for only the walls are plastered, and the summers and gist [joist?] are planed and kept very white scoured, as so is all the partitions if made of boards. The fireplaces have no jambs (as ours have) but the backs run flush with the walls, and the hearth is of tiles and is as far out into the room at the ends as before the

[32] An auction.

[33] New York still showed its Dutch origins in its population and architecture: tall houses with gabled ends to the street and frequently cobblestoned. It was about half as large as Boston, which had 7000 people, but it had no newspaper. Most of the inhabitants lived below Wall Street.

fire, which is generally five feet in the lower rooms, and the piece over where the mantle tree should be is made as ours with joiners' work, and as I suppose is fastened to iron rods inside. The house where the vendue was had chimney corners like ours, and they and the hearths were laid with the finest tile that I ever saw, which is ever clean and so are the walls of the kitchen, which had a brick floor. They were making great preparations to receive their governor, Lord Cornbury,[34] from the Jerseys, and for that end raised the militia to guard him on shore to the fort.

They are generally of the Church of England and have a New England gentleman for their minister, and a very fine church set out with all customary requisites.[35] There are also a Dutch and diverse conventicles, as they call them, viz. Baptist, Quakers, &c. They are not strict in keeping the sabbath as in Boston and other places where I had been, but seem to deal with great exactness as far as I see or deal with. They are sociable to one another and courteous and civil to strangers and fare well in their houses. The English go very fashionable in their dress. But the Dutch, especially the middling sort, differ from

[34] Not his initial arrival, as Edward Hyde, Viscount Cornbury (1661–1723) had been appointed governor in 1702 and arrived that spring. He owed his appointment to the fact that he was a first cousin of Queen Anne, since he had no talent except for dishonesty, oppression, and drinking. He was recalled in 1708.

[35] Trinity Church, chartered in 1697. The rector was the Rev. William Vesey.

our women, in their habit go loose, wear French *muches*[36] which are like a cap and a headband in one, leaving their ears bare, which are set out with jewels of a large size and many in number. And their fingers hooped with rings, some with large stones in them of many colors, as were their pendants in their ears, which you should see very old women wear as well as young.

They have vendues very frequently and make their earnings very well by them, for they treat with good liquor liberally, and the customers drink as liberally and generally pay for it as well by paying for that which they bid up briskly for, after the sack has gone plentifully about, though sometimes good penny worths are got there.

Their diversion in the winter is riding sleighs about three or four miles out of town, where they have houses of entertainment at a place called the Bowery; and some go to friends' houses who handsomely treat them. Mr. Burroughs carried his spouse and daughter and myself out to one Madam Dowe's, a gentlewoman that lived at a farm house, who gave us a handsome entertainment of five or six dishes and choice beer and metheglin,[37] cider, &c., all which she said was the produce of her farm. I believe we met 50 or 60 sleighs that day. They fly with great swiftness and some are so furious that they'll turn

---

[36] She must mean *mouchoirs*, the French word for handkerchiefs or kerchiefs used as bonnets.

[37] Mead, made from fermented honey and water.

out of the path for none except a laden cart. Nor do they spare any diversion the place affords, and sociable to a degree, their tables being as free to their neighbors as to themselves.

Having here transacted the affair I went upon and some other that fell in the way, after about a fortnight's stay there I left New York with no little regret, and Thursday, December 21, set out for New Haven with my kinsman Trowbridge and the man that waited on me about one [in the] afternoon, and about three came to a half-way house about ten miles out of town, where we baited and went forward; about 5 came to Spuyten Duyvil, else Kingsbridge,[38] where they pay three pence for passing over with a horse, which the man that keeps the gate set up at the end of the bridge receives.

We hoped to reach the French town [New Rochelle] and lodge there that night, but unhappily lost our way about four miles short, and being overtaken by a great storm of wind and snow which set full in our faces about dark, we were very uneasy. But meeting one Gardner, who lived in a cottage thereabout, [he] offered us his fire to sit by, having but one poor bed and his wife not well, &c., or he would go to a house with us, where he thought we might be better accommodated. Thither we went, but a surly old she creature, not worthy the name of

[38] Spuyten Duyvil Creek connects the Harlem and Hudson rivers, forming the northern boundary of Manhattan Island. Kingsbridge was the town on the north side.

woman, who would hardly let us go into her door, though the weather was so stormy none but she would have turned out a dog. But her son, whose name was Gallop, who lived just by invited us to his house and showed me two pair of stairs, viz. one up the loft and tother up the bed, which was as hard as it was high, and warmed it with a hot stone at the foot.

I lay very uncomfortably, insomuch that I was so very cold and sick I was forced to call them up to give me something to warm me. They had nothing but milk in the house, which they boiled, and to make it better sweetened it with molasses, which I not knowing or thinking of it till it was down and coming up again, which it did in so plentiful a manner that my host was soon paid double for his portion, and that in specie. But I believe it did me service in clearing my stomach. So after this sick and weary night at East Chester (a very miserable poor place), the weather being now fair, Friday the 22nd December we set out for New Rochelle, where being come we had good entertainment and recruited ourselves very well.

This is a very pretty place well compact, and good handsome houses, clean, good and passable roads, and situated on a navigable river, abundance of land well fined and cleared all along as we passed, which caused in me a love to the place, which I could have been content to live in it. Here we rode over a bridge made of one entire stone of such a breadth that a cart might pass with safety, and to spare. It lay over a passage cut through a rock to convey water to a mill not far off. Here are three fine taverns within call of each other, very good provision for travelers.

Thence we traveled through Mamaroneck, a neat though little place, with a navigable river before it, one of the pleasantest I ever saw. Here were good buildings, especially one, a very fine seat, which they told me was Col. Hethcoat's,[39] who I had heard was a very fine gentleman. From hence we came to Horseneck,[40] where we baited, and they told me that one Church of England parson officiated in all these three towns once every Sunday, in turns throughout the year; and that they all could but poorly maintain him, which they grudged to do, being a poor and quarrelsome crew as I understand by our host. Their quarreling about their choice of minister, they chose to have none, but caused the government to send this gentleman to them.

Here we took leave of New York government and descending the mountainous passage that almost broke my heart in ascending before, we came to Stamford, a well compact town, but miserable meeting house, which we passed, and through many and great difficulties, as bridges which were exceeding high and very tottering and of vast length, steep and

[39] Caleb Heathcote (1666–1721) was a prosperous New York merchant and militia colonel who moved to Westchester in 1696 and became its mayor. He owned a tract of 20 square miles running inland from Mamaroneck.

[40] Horseneck is now West Greenwich.

rocky hills and precipices (bug-bears to a fearful female traveler). About nine at night we came to Norwalk, having crept over a timber of a broken bridge about thirty feet long and perhaps fifty to the water. I was exceeding tired and cold when we came to our inn, and could get nothing there but poor entertainment and the impertinent babble of one of the worst of men, among many others of which our host made one, who had he been one degree impudenter would have outdone his grandfather. And this, I think, is the most perplexed night I have yet had.

*From hence Saturday, Dec. 23*, a very cold and windy day, after an intolerable night's lodging, we hasted forward only observing in our way the town to be situated on a navigable river, with indifferent buildings and people more refined than in some of the country towns we had passed, though vicious enough, the church and tavern being next neighbors.

Having ridden through a difficult river, we came to Fairfield, where we baited and were much refreshed as well with the good things which gratified our appetites as the time taken to rest our wearied limbs, which latter I employed in enquiring concerning the town and manners of the people, &c. This is a considerable town and filled as they say with wealthy people; have a spacious meeting house and good buildings. But the inhabitants are litigious, nor do they well agree with their minister, who (they say) is a very worthy gentleman.

They have abundance of sheep, whose very dung brings them great gain, with part of which they pay their parson's salary, and they grudge that, prefering their dung before their minister. They let out their sheep at so much as they agree upon for a night; the highest bidder always carries them. And they will sufficiently dung a large quantity of land before morning. But [they] were once bit by a sharper who had them a night and sheared them all before morning.

From hence we went to Stratford, the next town, in which I observed but few houses and those not very good ones. But the people that I conversed with were civil and good natured. Here we stayed till late at night, being to cross a dangerous river ferry, the river at that time full of ice; but after about four hours waiting with great difficulty we got over. My fears and fatigues prevented my here taking any particular observations. Being got to Milford, it being late in the night, I could go no farther. My fellow traveler going forward, I was invited to lodge at Mrs. _____, a very kind and civil gentlewoman, by whom I was handsomely and kindly entertained till the next night.

The people here go very plain in their apparel (more plain than I had observed in the towns I had passed) and seem to be very grave and serious. They told me there was a singing Quaker lived there, or at least had a strong inclination to be so; his spouse not at all affected that way. Some of the singing crew came there one day to visit him (to the woman's no small vexation), humming and singing and groaning after their conjuring way.

Says the woman, "Are you singing Quakers?"

"Yea," says they.

"Then take my squawling brat of a child here and sing to it," says she, "for I have almost split my throat with singing to him and can't get the rogue to sleep."

They took this as a great indignity and immediately departed. Shaking the dust from their heels, [they] left the good woman and her child among the number of the wicked.

This is a seaport place and accommodated with a good harbor, but I had not opportunity to make particular observations because it was sabbath day — [starting] this evening.

*December 24.*[41] I set out with the gentlewoman's son, whom she very civilly offered to go with me when she saw no persuasions would cause me to stay, which she pressingly desired; and crossing a ferry having but nine miles to New Haven, in a short time arrived there and was kindly received and well accommodated amongst my friends and relations.

The government of Connecticut colony begins westward towards York at Stamford (as I am told) and so runs eastward towards Boston (I mean in my range, because I don't intend to extend my description beyond my own travels) and ends that way at

[41] She must mean December 25.

Stonington. And had a great many large towns lying more northerly. It is a plentiful country for provisions of all sorts and it's generally healthy. No one that can and will be diligent in this place need fear poverty, nor the want of food and raiment.

*January 6th* [*1705*]. Being now well recruited and fit for business, I discoursed the persons I was concerned with that we might finish in order to [enable] my return to Boston. They delayed, as they had hitherto done, hoping to tire my patience. But I was resolute to stay and see an end of the matter, let it be never so much to my disadvantage. So January 9th they came again and promised the Wednesday following to go through with the distributions of the estate, which they delayed till Thursday and then came with new amusements. But at length by the mediation of that holy good gentleman, the Rev. Mr. James Pierpont,[42] the minister of New Haven, and with the advice and assistance of other our good friends, we came to an accommodation and distribution, which having finished, though not till February, the man that waited on me to York taking the charge of me, I set out for Boston.

We went from New Haven upon the ice (the ferry being not passable thereby), and the Rev. Mr. Pierpont with Madam Prout, Cousin Trowbridge,

[42] James Pierpont (1660–1714) graduated from Harvard in 1681 and began preaching at New Haven in 1684, where he remained the rest of his life. He was one of the founders of Yale.

and diverse others were taking leave, we went onward without anything remarkable till we came to New London and lodged again at Mr. Saltonstall's. And here I dismissed my guide, and my generous entertainer provided me Mr. Samuel Rogers of that place to go home with me. I stayed a day here longer than I intended by the commands of the Honorable Governor Winthrop to stay and take a supper with him, whose wonderful civility I may not omit.

The next morning I crossed the ferry to Groton, having had the honor of the company of Madam Livingston (who is the Governor's daughter)[43] and Mary Christophers and diverse others to the boat. And that night lodged at Stonington and had roast beef and pumpkin sauce for supper. The next night at Havens's and had roast fowl, and the next day we came to a river which by reason of the freshets coming down was swollen so high we feared it impassable, and the rapid stream was very terrifying. However, we must over and that in a small canoe. Mr. Rogers assuring me of his good conduct, I after a stay of near an hour on the shore for consultation went into the canoe, and Mr. Rogers paddled about 100 yards up the creek by the shore side, turned into the swift stream and dexterously steering her, in a moment

---

[43] Madam Livingston was Mary Winthrop, daughter of Gov. Fitz-John Winthrop. She died in January 1713, and Madam Knight married her daughter to the widower, Col. John Livingston, later in the same year.

we came to the other side as swiftly passing as an arrow shot out of the bow by a strong arm. I stayed on the shore till he returned to fetch our horses, which he caused to swim over, himself bringing the furniture in the canoe. But it is past my skill to express the exceeding fright all their transactions formed in me.

We were now in the colony of the Massachusetts, and taking lodgings at the first inn we came too, had a pretty difficult passage the next day, which was the second of March, by reason of the sloughy ways then thawed by the sun. Here I met Capt. John Richards of Boston who was going home, so being very glad of his company we rode something harder than hitherto, and missing my way in going up a very steep hill, my horse dropped down under me as dead. This new surprise no little hurt me, meeting it just at the entrance to Dedham from whence we intended to reach home that night. But was now obliged to get another horse there and leave my own, resolving for Boston that night, if possible. But in going over the causeway at Dedham, the bridge being overflowed by the high waters coming down, I very narrowly escaped falling over into the river, horse and all, which 'twas almost a miracle I did not.

Now it grew late in the afternoon and the people having very much discouraged us about the sloughy way, which they said we should find very difficult and hazardous, it so wrought on me, being tired and dispirited and disappointed of my desires of going home, that I agreed to lodge there that night, which we did at the house of one Draper.

*And the next day being March 3rd*, we got safe home to Boston, where I found my aged and tender mother and my dear and only child in good health, with open arms ready to receive me, and my kind relations and friends flocking in to welcome me and hear the story of my transactions and travels, I having this day been five months from home and now I cannot fully express my joy and satisfaction; but desire sincerely to adore my Great Benefactor for thus graciously carrying me forth and returning in safety His unworthy handmaid.

# 2

## The Present State of Louisiana

*

*French Life in New Orleans*
1743

# French Life in New Orleans
## 1743

*While the English were filling up the Atlantic seaboard of North America, the French were extending their thin lines of settlement on the St. Lawrence westward, and on the lower Mississippi northward. These two great waterways into the interior of the continent served as highways, but the nature and purpose of French colonization did not encourage the growth of cities or even towns. Interested almost exclusively in the fur trade, the French abhorred any idea of displacing the native Indians, whom they cultivated as suppliers. Hence, when in 1743 the English counted a white population of about 850,000 along the Atlantic from Florida to Nova Scotia, the French could not tally more than 50,000 in its two provinces of Canada and Louisiana.*

*Although Quebec was founded in 1608 and Montreal was settled in 1642, the Mississippi Valley was not claimed until La Salle paddled down the great river in 1682. He then went to France and obtained a charter from Louis XIV to establish a colony in Louisiana, but upon returning by ship through the Gulf of Mexico two years later he was unable to find the mouth of the Mississippi. War between*

France and England deferred further efforts at settlement, and it was not until 1699 that Iberville established some 200 colonists at Biloxi, followed by Bienville three years later with a post on Mobile Bay. The King lost interest in colonizing Louisiana as he undertook a second war in Europe. Then in 1718 the area was given over to a private company to exploit and develop. New Orleans was founded that year, and in 1722 was made the capital of the province. A few smaller posts were constructed to the northward, and a large group of German settlers was brought in. Yet the company went bankrupt and after several bad harvests and a bloody war with the Natchez Indians surrendered its charter in 1731, and Louisiana reverted to a royal colony. At that time it held a population of 5000 whites and 2000 blacks. In the next dozen years the number of whites declined.

The redoubtable Bienville was appointed governor in 1733 and ruled for ten years, during which time he fought the pro-English Chickasaws twice, finally wringing a peace treaty from them in 1740. By this time the French had a fort up the river at modern Memphis, three small posts in modern Indiana, and a cluster of villages around a fort in southern Illinois. The western reaches of Canada included settlements at Detroit, Mackinac Straits, and Green Bay. In other words, Louisiana and

*Canada were virtually connected at their interiors, and the two provinces formed a constrictive ring around the English colonies.*

*When Bienville went home to France in 1743, he may have been followed by an officer who wrote a descriptive and opinionated account of Louisiana. The author has never been identified, but either he or the recipient (if there was one) of his narrative got it published as "The Present State of the Country and Inhabitants, Europeans and Indians, of Louisiana . . . by an Officer at New Orleans to his Friend at Paris", London, 1744. It did not appear in France, probably because of its critical tone, and this fact might raise a question as its genuineness. It would appeal to Englishmen, who were then on the eve of a third war with France. Yet it contains no ascertainable falsehoods, and its reliability has not been repudiated. Indeed, "The Present State" was unknown to historians of Louisiana in the eighteenth and most of the nineteenth century. Justin Winsor, in his monumental "Narrative and Critical History of America," called attention to it in 1887 as a neglected source. It is a rare book and has not been reprinted until now, with the omission of four letters from Governor Vaudreuil, who succeeded Bienville, dated early in 1744, which form an appendix.*

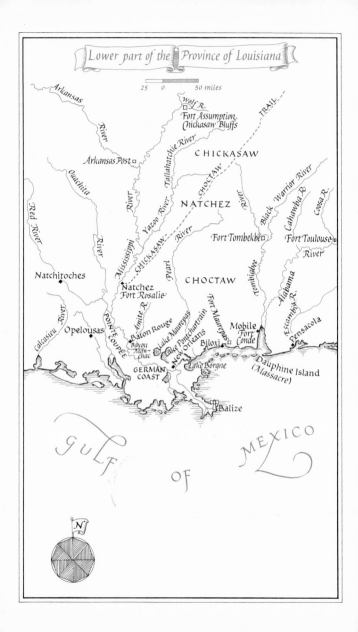

# The Present State of Louisiana

MONSIEUR DE LA SALLE, a Norman, was the first who discovered Louisiana, above 50 years ago. He got thither through Canada; that is, he went down the River Mississippi as far as the Gulf of Mexico, where it falls into the ocean. Before him the English had attempted to go up the river; but when they came to a certain winding, which forms a circle only 7 leagues below New Orleans, they conjectured, upon finding themselves much about the place from whence they departed the evening before, that they were got to the end could go no farther; whereupon they turned back. From hence this place is called *Detour des Anglois*.

Both the beginning and ending of that winding are, I think, to the east; so that in the space of two or three hours one has the sun both before and behind; and this it was that deceived the poor English. Monsieur de La Salle, who came down the Mississippi as far as the Gulf, went back the same way up to Canada; from whence he returned to France and made application to the king for a ship, in order to complete the discovery of this country, which was accordingly granted to him. By this means the Louisiana belongs to the French.

The country was found inhabited all along the Mississippi by small savage nations who had no manner of knowledge of the French. They might,

however, have seen or heard talk of white men, because the English, and after them the French had
discovered and taken possession of the Island of
Mobile, which is called Fort Condé. Ten leagues
from thence, upon the sea shore, stands Fort
Dauphine, which is called Massacre because the
savages destroyed and massacred at that place an
infinite number of the English.[1] One hundred leagues
from Mobile, going up a river of the same name, is
a port called Tombekbé, where there is a commanding officer and a garrison. Above 100 leagues from
Mobile, pursuing the course of the river of the
Alibamons, stands Fort Toulouse, where is likewise
a commanding officer and a garrison.

These countries are inhabited by the Chickasaws,
a savage nation against whom we have hitherto
stood upon our guard; but we are now treating
about peace with them. They are quitting the side
of the English, and Mons. Vaudreuil[2] is just gone to
Mobile to treat with their chiefs and to receive their
presents and give them others; for these gentry make
presents *pilla*, that is gratis, provided presents are
also made to them. There we have also the Choctaws, or Flatheads, about 5000 men fit to bear arms,
who are our great friends and declared enemies of

[1] Dauphine Island, outside the entrance to Mobile Bay,
was first called Massacre Island because when Iberville visited
it in 1699 he found a great quantity of human bones, but
there is no reason to think that they were English bones.

[2] The new governor, Pierre de Rigaud de Vaudreuil, who
reached New Orleans early in 1743.

the Chickasaws, whose friends they will become if peace is concluded. They are called Choctaws because their heads are really flat, occasioned by this: that as soon as they are born and during their infancy, their heads are bound very tight with bandages, insomuch that they can look up perpendicularly without lifting up their heads.[3]

I shall slightly pass over these cantons because I have not been among them; I only know that the way to them is through the Lake of Ponchartrain, which lies a league from New Orleans to the northward. It is easy to conclude that the nations which the French found along the Mississippi did not carry on any commerce: they dwelt as they do still in wooden cabins very ill built and distant enough from each other and do not appear like cities or towns; they call them villages.

The custom is to travel on the river, it not being possible to make long journeys by land, because of the bad roads, morasses that must be traversed, thick forest, and the difficulty of finding victuals, though wild oxen, kids, and wild fowl might be found. But then, as there could be no other way of going than on foot, a man could not carry a sufficient quantity of powder and shot. It would be more easy for the savages, who walk very well in the woods and esteem it but a small matter to live several days

[3] Probably an exaggeration, as the brow was little affected. The practice was found among several tribes but not, strangely enough, among the tribe which is today called Flathead.

without eating; but they nevertheless perform their journeys by water, excepting the Chickasaws, who are much afraid of it.

We have an open trade with the Spaniards and Americans; by Americans I mean the merchants who come from St. Domingo and Martinique by sea. There is no going into America by the River Mississippi, the source of which is not discovered; and it is navigated upon no farther than from the sea as high as the Red River, 200 leagues from New Orleans, where one leaves it to go to the Natchez; and from thence by other rivers as far as the Illinois; from whence one goes on to Canada partly by land and partly by water. In order to do so, canoes are made of the bark of trees which are bound with twigs and which two men carry where there is a footway; and you get into them to cross any morasses, lakes, or bays which intervene. I have never been this journey and therefore speak of it only from hearsay.

Heretofore we traded with the Spaniards, to whom we carried proper merchandises for which they paid in good piastres; but Monsieur Vaudreuil has forbid carrying any more to them; if they want us, they must come to us. It is to be presumed that he has sufficient reasons for hindering these voyages.

We trade at present with the Americans, to whom for their stuffs and rum we give piastres or other goods, chiefly peas and beans, which are very rare especially at Martinico; we also supply them with timber for building ships. To the merchants who bring stuffs, cloth, wine, brandy, liquors, arms, and meal from France, we give in exchange tobacco, rice, *mahis*,[4] cotton, indigo, skins, pine wood, cypress, cedar, log wood, pitch, tar, or piastres, paper bills having no currency but in the colony. We do also give them bills of exchange. Lastly we supply the savages with fusils,[5] powder, shot, knives, needles, razors, vermillion, woollen, ribbons, blankets, shirts, blue and red cloth, and brandy well mixed with water; for which we get skins of wild oxen, kids, otters, beavers, venison, or wild fowl and whatever else they can get that pleases. These also, who come often to New Orleans, take paper notes in payment.

The French live sociably enough, but the officers are too free with the town's people; and the town's people that are rich are too proud and lofty. Their inferiors hardly dare to speak to them, and here as everywhere else [to make use of a common proverb] an upstart fellow thinks that others are not worthy to look at him. Every one studies his own profit; the poor labor for a week and squander in one day all they have earned in six; from thence arises the profit of the public houses, which flourish every day. The rich spend their time in seeing their slaves work to improve their lands, and get money which they

---

[4] Maize, or Indian corn. The piastre was the old Spanish peso, or dollar.

[5] Flintlock muskets.

spend in plays, balls, and feasts. But the most common pastime of the highest as well as lowest, and even of the slaves, is women; so that if there are 500 women married or unmarried in New Orleans, including all ranks, I don't believe without exaggeration that there are ten of them of a blameless character; as for me, I know but two of those and even they are privately talked of. What I say of New Orleans, I say of the whole province, without being guilty of slander or calumny. Laws are observed here much in the same manner as in France, or worse: the rich man knows how to procure himself justice of the poor, if the affair is to his advantage; but if the poor man is in the right, he is obliged to enter into a composition; if the rich is in the wrong the affair is stifled. They deal fairly with such as are very sharp-sighted. As the king is at a great distance, they make him provide victuals, arms, and clothing for the troops, which those who keep the offices or magazines sell and put the money in their own pockets; the poor soldier for whom they were designed never so much as seeing them.

Let us now take a view of what relates to the table. Those who have not much money are seldom without wine in their cellars; the tradesman is seldom a week without drinking it beyond moderation; but that is nothing in comparison with the soldier. . . . That the reader may the better comprehend the expense of his way of living, I shall set down the price the soldier pays for eatables and drinkables at a tavern. Liquors are a pistole a bottle; brandy, three livres fifteen sols;[6] rum and wine, fifty sols; bread, twelve sols a pound; butcher's meat, six sols; a sucking pig, 100 sols; a turkey, three or four livres; a goose, fifty sols; a duck, twenty-five; a teal, twelve; a small salad, thirty; and if one will pass a quarter of an hour with a female, white, red, black, or tawny, you must reckon upon a bill of fifty sols. . . .

In the upper part of the country, towards the Illinois, besides wine and brandy they have a wild grape with which they make, as I am told, a small sourish wine. They also extract a syrup from a certain tree, which is called *erable*,[7] by making incisions therein out of which this syrup runs, without damaging the tree; and 'tis a very good liquor by report of those who have tasted it. There is wheat also among the Illinois, but not enough to supply the province with flour. There is meat at the shambles[8] every day: beef, veal, and mutton. Wild beef and all sorts of wild fowl are only eaten in the winter, but that does not prevent the killing meat constantly at the shambles. Pork is also a common food; everybody rears it, even the slaves, and they rear fowls also.

[6] A pistole was a French coin worth about $2; a livre was worth about 20 cents. Twenty sols or sous equaled one livre. Farther on the reader will see denier: twelve of them equaled one sol.

[7] The sugar maple tree.

[8] A place for slaughtering animals or selling slaughtered animals.

As the ground is very soft, a plow is seldom used, but it is dug by the slaves; and those whose ground is hard enough for the plow make use of oxen; they are also used in the carriages, the horses being only fit for riding and even for that they are but little esteemed, they are so small.

Louisiana in its full extent contains about 800 leagues of country, but it is far from all inhabited. I have mentioned above the posts to the east of Mobile. Let us now begin at the mouth of the River Mississippi. There is a fort to the eastward by the sea side called Balize, where there is a commanding officer and a garrison and by which ships enter into the river. Thirty leagues[9] from Balize one begins to find habitations on both sides the river, at the distance of a league or two from each other. It is ten leagues from the first habitation to New Orleans; the habitations above that place are half a league or leagues from each other. Ten leagues above the town is a post, the Germans, because inhabited by German families; there is a French commanding officer and a small garrison.

Thirty leagues higher is Pointe Coupée, where there is a commanding officer and a small garrison, with some inhabitants. One hundred leagues higher are the Natchez, which about twenty years ago was the best settled part of the colony; but the savages,

[9] At this time in America, a league was considered to be about three miles. Hence, thirty leagues were approximately ninety of our miles.

who gave name to that country, revolted and in the night surprised and either massacred or burnt the Frenchmen and made all the women slaves. Perhaps the reader won't be sorry to have an account of their cruelty, which I have learnt from some of those women who now live at New Orleans and with whom I am well acquainted.[10]

The barbarous Natchez regarded neither age nor sex; they burnt at cadre all the men whom they took alive. They destroyed the children and the women with child, whom they looked upon as an encumbrance, and made slaves of the others, among whom were several officers' wives. Those poor wretches suffered unheard of torments; the most cruel of which was being forced to yield to the brutish passions of their masters. What more shocking for a Christian and virtuous woman! They were employed in carrying water, cutting and carrying wood, pounding *mahis*, making *sagamité*[11] and baking it. They had nothing to live upon but the scraps which those monsters of nature threw to them, as to

[10] The Natchez attack on Fort Rosalie occurred on Nov. 28, 1729. The Indians killed the commanding officer and all the men, about 250 in number, burned the fort, and carried off the women. With the help of the Choctaws, the French attacked the Natchez in March 1730 and recovered the women captives, but most of the Natchez escaped. In another expedition late in the year the French captured the Natchez chief and 427 others, whom they sold into slavery. More of them were killed in 1731, and the remnant took refuge among the Chickasaws.

[11] A mush of maize, or corn boiled in salt water.

dogs, and so little that what supported them for a day was hardly sufficient for one meal. In this condition those unfortunate Frenchwomen remained for two or three years [actually, months], exposed to be cruelly beaten for the slightest faults. They were at last ransomed, but some of them carrying with the female sex a manly heart and courage saved themselves by killing their tyrants. By degrees the Natchez were destroyed; however, there are still a few of them left among the Chickasaws, whom these last promised to give up alive or dead.

This post [Fort Rosalie] is towards the north and has a commanding officer and a garrison, with three or four inhabitants. From thence comes the best tobacco of the country. The soil is very good and very agreeable, there being prodigious fine meadows and mountains, insomuch that it looks like a little France. From thence the course of the river leads to the south, where you find the Natchitoches, from whom you proceed to New Mexico, where there are mines of gold dust. To go from the Natchez to the Illinois and to Canada, you must quit the River Mississippi and enter upon the Red River;[12] and from that upon others where you find the Tunicas, the Arkansas, the Attacapas, the Avoyelles, the Kaskaskias, and the Illinois, and higher up the Panis, the Nicanies, the Missouris, the Weas, the River Wabash, &c.

[12]The author's geography is confused. He does not seem to know that the Illinois settlements were on the Mississippi.

The country of the Illinois is full of mountains, from which they get stones for building houses. There is a commanding officer and two companies of 50 men each who supply the neighboring posts. The Illinois lie far to the north, facing the Gulf of Mexico; so that if one could go thither from Balize directly across the woods without going up the Mississippi, it would save near 400 leagues. There are iron and lead mines among the Illinois. They make salt in leaden kettles and get water for it out of the neighboring lakes, which are saltish.[13]

As to what relates to game, it is open and allowed to everybody, it not being possible to make inclosures in the woods where the game haunt. The dearness of the bread, worth 16 sols 8 deniers a pound, that country money does not hinder the poor from eating it, though they make some rice, which is much cheaper and is the ordinary food of the low sort of people. The slaves are fed with rice, or with *mahis* husked and boiled, which is called *sagamité*.

We have no proper fairs; the slaves are sold from one person to another, or by auction. There are very few savage slaves, because we are at peace with all the nations; those we have were taken in former wars and we keep them. Our Negroes are procured from the [West India] Islands, or from Guinea.

Perhaps the reader will be glad to know what we do with our paper notes when they are much worn.

[13] He must mean salt springs or marshes.

We sew them up, or when they are too old, we carry them back to the treasury and get new ones.[14]

The forces are pretty well kept; they have a complete clothing every two years, and part of a clothing every year; but 'tis not very faithfully distributed, for out of three clothings the commissaries make shift to get one. They have pretty fine ammunition, bread one-half pound a day, and ten pounds of salt pork a month. The money to be paid them after deducting off-reckonings comes to 29 sols, 6 deniers per month, which the King directs to be paid in French money; but instead of that, they give them paper notes, which amount only to 14 sols, 9 deniers of France; the rest goes into the commissaries' pockets.

The country was at first settled by lewd, good-for-nothing people sent from France by force; afterwards by young people who went thither by choice; and by young people who had no fathers, taken with their own goodwill out of the hospitals at Paris and L'Orient. At present no women are sent there against their will. Sometimes false coiners and smugglers are sent thither, but they are free in the country and work for themselves; and even those of them who choose to enter among the troops are received there, provided they have not passed through the hands of justice.

[14] Hard money was so scarce the inhabitants used home-made card currency to settle debts. When worn, it was exchanged locally for new cards. It was not accepted in France, of course.

The mechanic arts flourish. The King sends workmen for building and repairing his ships. He entertains seamen there, and workmen in wood and iron. As this country belongs to the King, the Company has no office there; however, they keep an agent who pays himself out of old debts and enriches himself, though the Company gets little.

The youth here are employed in hunting, fishing, and pleasuring. Very few learn the necessary sciences, or at best it is what is least attended to. The children, even of the best sort, know how to fire a musket or shoot an arrow, catch fish, draw a bow, handle an oar, swim, run, dance, play at cards, and understand paper notes before they know their letters or their God. A child of six years of age knows more here of raking and swearing than a young man of 25 in France; and an insolent boy of 12 or 13 years of age will boldly insult and strike an old man.

The different ranks of people here are the Governor, the Commissary Director (for he has not the title of Intendant), the King's lieutenant, the major, the military officers, the Council, the officers of the Quil, the militia officers, the troops, and the people.

I desire the reader to consider that I do not pretend to give this as a studied piece; my design is to gratify the curiosity of some persons who have done me the honor to desire an account of the country where I am, which I have done plainly and ingeniously. As to the manners and customs of the

people, I relate them as they are; and if any part
seems satirical, it does not proceed from malice; I
could not suppress it without betraying the truth.
I might, indeed, have a little more spared those
whom I find occasion to censure; but I speak my
mind freely, and like another Despreaux[15] (the
comparison is a little rash) I give everything its
proper appelation; and I do positively affirm that in
this country.

> A disregard to heaven's shown; the judges partial
> are:
> Honesty is quite despised; and common are the
> fair.

Though I have so little indulgence for others, I beg
my readers to have some for me, and upon account
of my sincerity honor me with their favor.

[15]Nicolas Boileau-Despreaux (1656–1711), French poet
and critic, who satirized his contemporaries and became
known for his frankness and harsh literary criticism.

# 3

## Life and Travels of Col. James Smith

*

*An Indian Captive in Ohio*
1755–60

# An Indian Captive in Ohio
## 1755–60

*James Smith is the eighteenth-century personification of the American frontiersman, although not as well known as Daniel Boone or Simon Kenton. Born in 1737, Smith was on the frontier when it was the Appalachian Mountains. He grew up in central Pennsylvania and was captured by some Ohio Indians in 1755 at the age of eighteen. His life was spared and he was adopted into a Delaware-Caughnewaga village. Under Indian tutelage he grew self-sufficient in the wilderness, and the simple rhythm of savage life continually challenged him. He was not unschooled and he showed a great facility for languages as well as aptness for woods lore. Smith adapted to his family, hunted in neighborhood parties, and joined in the life of the village. His five years of captivity were spent in northern Ohio, with three visits to the Detroit River, and finally a journey to Montreal.*

*Ordinarily a memoir of events that happened forty years earlier is suspect and unreliable, but Smith said he kept a journal while a prisoner and retained it through the years. Further, he is recalling mainly what happened to him, and his*

73

*experiences burned deep into his memory. Indeed, he viewed his captors with less distaste and revulsion than he might have if he had written his narrative immediately on his return to civilization at age twenty-three. As it was, he looked back from his six- ties with a certain mellowed tolerance for and a better understanding of the Indians, who were try- ing with diminishing success to maintain a prim- itive culture on the cutting edge of a more powerful civilization. Since he had survived and prospered, he was not bitter or condescending.*

*Smith's relation vividly reveals the harshness and cruelty and lack of self-discipline in Indian life— the torture and killing of prisoners, the uncontrol- lable addiction to hard liquor when it could be pur- chased, the alternate seasons of feasting and famine, the carefree laziness until want forced exertion, fierceness in war as the mark of greatness. Yet he saw virtues in his companions, too: courage, kindness to one another, generous hospitality and sharing of food, occasional adoption of prisoners, thoughtful criticism of traders and missionaries. The reader will perceive that young Smith rather enjoyed the outdoor life of the Indians, and despite having been forcibly removed from a girl he loved he made no effort to escape from his captors for five years. But he never renounced his heritage to live the complete Indian life.*

*Capture by Indians is one fearful fate we no longer face, yet from the earliest settlements in America down to the Civil War, this danger was a normal hazard of expansion. Hundreds, perhaps thousands, suffered the hardships and cruelties of enslavement by Indians, and usually after the prisoners had seen other members of their families slaughtered. It lurked as a shuddering fear in every frontier cabin. Escaped or ransomed captives sometimes published an account of their experience, starting a distinct type of American literature. It became so popular in the nineteenth century that fictional "captivities" appeared on the market. But Smith's relation remains one of the best written and and most detailed narratives of captive life. A few anecdotes of hunting and fishing have been omitted, as well as subsequent episodes in his life in Pennsylvania.*

*After his return home and his marriage in 1763, Smith retained a liking for active life and adventure. Laws tended to be fetters for him. He raised a company of militia to defend the border from echoes of Pontiac's rebellion in 1763. The next year as a lieutenant he accompanied Col. Henry Bouquet on his expedition into Ohio to recover white captives and bring the Indians to terms. As trade with the western tribes revived, the first goods sent to them were arms and powder, which aroused the resent-*

ment of the frontiersmen. Smith led a small party
that intercepted a trader's train, shot the packhorses,
and burned the goods. When the commanding
officer at Fort Loudon arrested innocent men on
suspicion, again Smith raised a troop that seized
some British soldiers and traded them for release
of his friends.

After the region south of the Ohio River was
opened to settlement in 1766, Smith and three other
men set out for the Holston River in modern Ten-
nessee to select land for purchase. Smith parted
from his friends and returned through North Carolina and Virginia, nearly losing his life from an
injury that disabled him.

Again in 1769 frontier settlers tried to prevent
traders from arming hostile Indians and plundered
their goods. Several of them were arrested and put
in the guardhouse at Fort Bedford. With eighteen
followers Smith invaded the fort and rescued the
prisoners. Subsequently he was arrested, tried, and
acquitted. Smith was commissioned a captain of
Pennsylvania militia in 1774 at the time Virginia's
Governor Dunmore made war against the Ohio
Indians. In 1776 he was appointed a major, but
served in the provincial Assembly instead until
Washington invaded New Jersey at the beginning
of 1777. Smith then saw active service as a scout
and became a militia colonel the next year in
western Pennsylvania.

*His first wife died and left him with several children. In 1785 he married a widow, Margaret Rodgers Irvin, in Kentucky. They settled in Bourbon County, near Paris, and Smith represented the county in the General Assembly. He wrote his narrative in the 1790's, possibly at the insistence of his literary wife. As autobiography it has little balance, omitting his early years and late years; more than half of the book is devoted to his five years among the Indians. It was published at Lexington, Kentucky, by the state's first printer, John Bradford, in 1799 as "An Account of the Remarkable Occurrences in the Life and Travels of Colonel James Smith . . ." When it was reprinted in 1831 in Philadelphia, the editor believed that not more than a dozen copies of the first edition could be found. Today fewer copies than that are known, and they are rarities in the $10,000 to $12,000 class. The second edition evidently met with a good reception because it was reprinted in 1834. The book was republished again in 1870 and 1907.*

*Smith's second wife died in 1800. At the outbreak of the War of 1812 he issued a manual on how to fight Indians called "A Treatise on the Mode and Manner of Indian War," which included material from his earlier work. Smith died in Washington County, Kentucky, in 1812 esteemed as an exemplary Christian and an unwavering patriot, according to friends.*

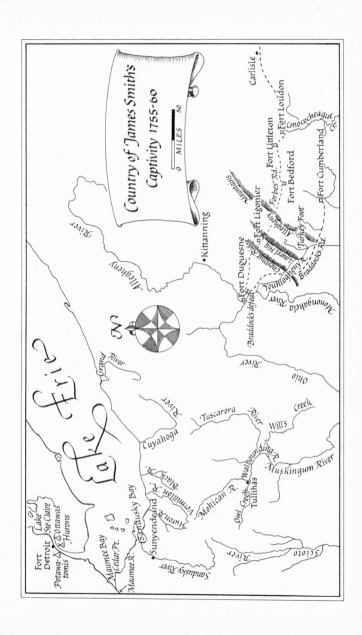

Country of James Smith's Captivity 1755-60

# An Account of
# the Remarkable Occurrences
# in the Life and Travels
# of Col. James Smith

IN May 1755 the Province of Pennsylvania agreed
to send out three hundred men in order to cut a
wagon road from Fort Loudon to join Braddock's
road near the Turkey Foot, or three forks of Yoho-
gania.[1] My brother-in-law, William Smith, Esq. of
Conococheague, was appointed commissioner to
have the oversight of these road cutters.

Though I was at that time only eighteen years of
age, I had fallen violently in love with a young lady
whom I apprehended was possessed of a large share
of both beauty and virtue; but being born between
Venus and Mars, I concluded I must also leave my
dear fair one and go out with this company of road
cutters to see the event of this campaign; but still

---

[1] As the Youghiogheny River flows northward out of Maryland, it turns in southern Pennsylvania and is joined by two
creeks (Confluence, Pa.) so the three streams resemble a
turkey foot. Just below this juncture Gen. Braddock was
expected to pass from Cumberland toward Pittsburgh. From
Fort Loudon, which is on Conococheague Creek, the new
road was being cut through Bedford and then would curve
southward to the Turkey Foot. It was not finished then.

expecting that some time in the course of the summer I should again return to the arms of my beloved.

We went on with the road without interruption until near the Allegheny Mountain,[2] when I was sent back in order to hurry up some provision wagons that were on the way after us. I proceeded down the road as far as the crossings of Juniata [River], where, finding the wagons were coming on as fast as possible, I returned up the road again towards Allegheny Mountain in company with one Arnold Vigoras. About four or five miles above Bedford three Indians had made a blind of bushes stuck in the ground, as though they grew naturally, where they concealed themselves about fifteen yards from the road. When we came opposite to them, they fired upon us at this short distance and killed my fellow traveller, yet their bullets did not touch me; but my horse making a violent start threw me, and the Indians immediately ran up and took me prisoner. The one that laid hold on me was a Canasatauga,[3] the other two were Delawares. One of them could speak English and asked me if there were any more white men coming after? I told them not any near that I knew of. Two of these Indians stood by me while the other scalped my comrade; they then set off and ran at a smart rate through the woods for

[2] Allegheny Mountain is a high ridge west of Bedford.

[3] Probably a Conestoga, one of a declining and displaced branch of Iroquois living on the Susquehanna River. The capture took place on July 3, 1755.

about fifteen miles, and that night we slept on the Allegheny Mountain without fire.

The next morning they divided the last of their provision which they had brought from Fort Duquesne and gave me an equal share, which was about two or three ounces of mouldy biscuit; this and a young ground-hog, about as large as a rabbit, roasted and also equally divided, was all the provision we had until we came to the Loyal Hannon,[4] which was about fifty miles; and a great part of the way we came through exceeding rocky laurel thickets without any path.

When we came to the west side of Laurel Hill,[5] they gave the scalp halloo as usual, which is a long yell or halloo for every scalp or prisoner they have in possession; the last of these scalp halloos was followed with quick and sudden shrill shouts of joy and triumph. On their performing this, we were answered by the firing of guns on the Loyal Hannon one after another, quicker then one could count, by another party of Indians who were encamped near where Ligonier now stands.[6] As we advanced near this party, they increased with re-

[4] Loyal Hannon, or Loyalhanna Creek, rises near modern Stahlstown and flows northeast toward Ligonier, near which it turns northwest and then north, emptying into the Kiskiminetas River at Saltsburg.

[5] He means Laurel Mountain, which rises on the border between Somerset and Westmoreland counties, just east of Ligonier.

[6] Ligonier, which did not exist in 1755, is about 40 miles west of Bedford.

peated shouts of joy and triumph; but I did not share with them in their excessive mirth. When we came to this camp, we found they had plenty of turkeys and other meat there, and though I never before ate venison without bread or salt yet as I was hungry, it relished very well. There we lay that night, and the next morning the whole of us marched on our way for Fort Duquesne.[7]

The night after, we joined another camp of Indians with nearly the same ceremony, attended with great noise and apparent joy among all, except one. The next morning we continued our march, and in the afternoon we came in full view of the fort, which stood on the point near where Fort Pitt now stands. We then made a halt on the bank of the Allegheny and repeated the scalp halloo, which was answered by the firing of all the firelocks in the hands of both Indians and French who were in and about the fort, in the aforesaid manner, and also the great guns, which were followed by the continued shouts and yells of the different savage tribes who were then collected there.

As I was at this time unacquainted with this mode of firing and yelling of the savages, I concluded that there were thousands of Indians there ready to receive General Braddock; but what added to my surprise, I saw numbers running towards me stripped naked excepting breech clouts, and painted in the

[7] Fort Duquesne was the French fort, just built, on the site of Pittsburgh.

most hideous manner of various colors, though the principal color was vermillion or a bright red; yet there was annexed to this black, brown, blue, &c. As they approached they formed themselves into two long ranks about two or three rods apart. I was told by an Indian that could speak English that I must run between these ranks, and that they would flog me all the way as I ran; and if I ran quick it would be so much the better, as they would quit when I got to the end of the ranks.

There appeared to be a general rejoicing around me, yet I could find nothing like joy in my breast; but I started to the race with all the resolution and vigor I was capable of exerting and found that it was as I had been told, for I was flogged the whole way. When I got near the end of the lines, I was struck with something that appeared to me to be a stick, or the handle of a tomahawk, which caused me to fall to the ground. On my recovering my senses I endeavored to renew my race; but as I arose someone cast sand in my eyes which blinded me so that I could not see where to run. They continued beating me most intolerably until I was at length insensible; but before I lost my senses I remember my wishing to strike the fatal blow, for I thought they intended killing me, but apprehended they were too long about it.

The first thing I remember was my being in the fort, amid the French and Indians, and a French doctor standing by me who had opened a vein in my left arm; after which the interpreter asked me how I did.

I told him I felt much pain. The doctor then washed my wounds and the bruised places of my body with French brandy. As I felt faint and the brandy smelt well, I asked for some inwardly, but the doctor told me by the interpreter that it did not suit my case.

When they found I could speak, a number of Indians came around me and examined me with threats of cruel death if I did not tell the truth. The first question they asked me was, how many men were there in the party that was coming from Pennsylvania to join Braddock? I told them the truth, that there were three hundred. The next question was, were they well armed? I told them they were all well armed (meaning the arm of flesh), for they had only thirty guns among the whole of them, which, if the Indians had known, they would certainly have gone and cut them all off. Therefore I could not in conscience let them know the defenseless situation of these road cutters. I was then sent to the hospital and carefully attended by the doctors and recovered quicker than what I expected.

Some time after I was there I was visited by the Delaware Indian already mentioned, who was at the taking of me and could speak some English. Though he spoke but bad English, yet I found him to be a man of considerable understanding. I asked him if I had done anything that had offended the Indians, which caused them to treat me so unmercifully. He said no, it was only an old custom the Indians had, and it was like "how do you do." After that, he said, I would be well used. I asked him if I should be admitted to remain with the French? He said no, and told me that as soon as I recovered I must not only go with the Indians but must be made an Indian myself. I asked him what news from Braddock's army? He said the Indians spied them every day, and he showed me by making marks on the ground with a stick that Braddock's army was advancing in very close order, and that the Indians would surround them, take trees, and (as he expressed it) "shoot um down all one pigeon."

Shortly after this, on the 9th day of July, 1755, in the morning, I heard a great stir in the fort. As I could then walk with a staff in my hand, I went out of the door, which was just by the wall of the fort, and stood upon the wall and viewed the Indians in a huddle before the gate, where were barrels of powder, bullets, flints, &c., and everyone taking what suited. I also saw the Indians march off in rank entire, likewise the French Canadians and some regulars. After viewing the Indians and French in different positions, I computed them to be about four hundred and wondered that they attempted to go out against Braddock with so small a party.[8] I was then in high hopes that I would soon see them fly before the British troops, and that General Braddock would take the fort and rescue me.

[8] It is now believed that the force sent to strike Braddock's expedition consisted of 290 French regulars and Canadian militia, and more than 600 Indians.

I remained anxious to know the event of this day; and in the afternoon I again observed a great noise and commotion in the fort and though at that time I could not understand French, yet I found that it was the voice of joy and triumph and feared that they had received what I called bad news.

I had observed some of the old country soldiers speak Dutch. As I spoke Dutch, I went to one of them and asked him, what was the news? He told me that a runner had just arrived who said that Braddock would certainly be defeated; that the Indians and French had surrounded him and were concealed behind trees and gullies and kept a constant fire upon the English; and that they saw the English falling in heaps and if they did not take the river, which was the only gap, and make their escape, there would not be one man left alive before sundown. Some time after this I heard a number of scalp halloos and saw a company of Indians and French coming in. I observed they had a great many bloody scalps, grenadiers' caps, British canteens, bayonets, &c. with them. They brought the news that Braddock was defeated. After that another company came in which appeared to be about one hundred, and chiefly Indians, and it seemed to me that almost every one of this company was carrying scalps. After this came another company with a number of wagon horses and also a great many scalps. Those that were coming in and those that had arrived kept a constant firing of small arms and also the great guns in the fort, which were accompanied with the most hideous shouts and yells from all quarters, so that it appeared to me as if the infernal regions had broke loose.

About sundown I beheld a small party coming with about a dozen prisoners, stripped naked, with their hands tied behind their backs and their faces and part of their bodies blacked. These prisoners were burned to death on the bank of Allegheny River opposite to the fort. I stood on the fort wall until I beheld them begin to burn one of these men: they had him tied to a stake and kept touching him with fire-brands, red-hot irons, &c., and he screaming in a most doleful manner, the Indians in the meantime yelling like infernal spirits. As this scene appeared too shocking for me to behold, I retired to my lodgings both sore and sorry.

When I came into my lodgings I saw Russel's *Seven Sermons*,[9] which they had brought from the field of battle, which a Frenchman made a present to me. From the best information I could receive there were only seven Indians and four French killed in this battle, and five hundred British lay dead in the field, besides what were killed in the river on their retreat.[10]

The morning after the battle I saw Braddock's artillery brought into the fort. The same day I also

[9]The Englishman Robert Russel's *Seven Sermons* was immensely popular and had already reached 45 editions.

[10]Of Braddock's 1450 troops, almost 1000 were killed, captured, or wounded. The French and Indians are believed to have suffered fewer than 60 casualties. The battle took place a few miles southeast of Fort Duquesne on the Monongahela River.

saw several Indians in British officers' dress, with sash, half moon,[11] laced hats, &c., which the British then wore.

A few days after this the Indians demanded me, and I was obliged to go with them. I was not yet well able to march, but they took me in a canoe up the Allegheny River to an Indian town that was on the north side of the river, about forty miles above Fort Duquesne.[12] Here I remained about three weeks and was then taken to an Indian town on the west branch of Muskingum, about twenty miles above the forks, which was called Tullihas,[13] inhabited by Delawares, Caughnewagas,[14] and Mohicans. On our route between the aforesaid towns the country was chiefly black oak and white oak land, which appeared generally to be good wheat land, chiefly second and third rate intermixed with some rich bottoms.

[11] British officers were usually distinguished by crimson sashes around their waist and a silver gorget on the chain around their neck. It was engraved with the King's arms and the number of the regiment.

[12] Probably Kittaning, a large settlement of Delawares, Caughnewagas, and Iroquois near the site of the present town of Kittaning.

[13] Tullihas was located at the point where Owl Creek and the Mohican River united to form the Walhonding River, which is what Smith calls the West branch of the Muskingum. The town was about half way between modern Coshocton and Mt. Vernon.

[14] Caughnewagas were a remnant of an Iroquois tribe settled mainly on the St. Lawrence at Sault St. Louis, near Montreal, where they had been drawn and Christianized by the Jesuits. A few were scattered in Ohio and western Pennsylvania.

The day after my arrival at the aforesaid town, a number of Indians collected about me, and one of them began to pull the hair out of my head. He had some ashes on a piece of bark in which he frequently dipped his fingers in order to take the firmer hold, and so he went on as if he had been plucking a turkey until he had all the hair clean out of my head, except a small spot about three or four inches square on my crown. This they cut off with a pair of scissors, excepting three locks which they dressed up in their own mode. Two of these they wrapped round with a narrow beaded garter made by themselves for that purpose, and the other they plaited at full length and then stuck it full of silver brooches.

After this they bored my nose and ears and fixed me off with earrings and nose jewels. Then they ordered me to strip off my clothes and put on a breech-clout, which I did. They then painted my head, face, and body in various colors. They put a large belt of wampum on my neck, and silver bands on my hands and right arm; and so an old chief led me out in the street and gave the alarm halloo — *coo-wigh* — several times repeated quickly, and on this all that were in the town came running and stood round the old chief, who held me by the hand in the midst. As I at this time knew nothing of their mode of adoption and had seen them put to death all they had taken, and as I never could find that they saved a man alive at Braddock's defeat, I made no doubt but they were about putting me to death in some cruel manner.

The old chief, holding me by the hand, made a long speech, very loud, and when he had done he handed me to three squaws, who led me by the hand down the bank into the river until the water was up to our middle. The squaws then made signs to me to plunge myself into the water, but I did not understand them. I thought that the result of the council was that I should be drowned, and that these young ladies were to be the executioners. They all three laid violent hold of me, and I for some time opposed them with all my might, which occasioned loud laughter by the multitude that were on the bank of the river. At length one of the squaws made out to speak a little English (for I believe they began to be afraid of me) and said, "No hurt you." On this I gave myself up to their ladyships, who were as good as their word; for though they plunged me under water and washed and rubbed me severely, yet I could not say they hurt me much.

These young women then led me up to the council house, where some of the tribe were ready with new clothes for me. They gave me a new ruffled shirt which I put on, also a pair of leggings done off with ribbons and beads, likewise a pair of moccasins and garters dressed with beads, porcupine quills, and red hair; also a tinsel laced cappo. They again painted my head and face with various colors and tied a bunch of red feathers to one of those locks they had left on the crown of my head, which stood up five or six inches. They seated me on a bearskin and gave me a pipe, tomahawk, and pole-cat skin pouch, which had been skinned pocket fashion and contained tobacco, killegenico (dry sumac leaves), which they mix with their tobacco; also spunk,[15] flint, and steel.

When I was thus seated, the Indians came dressed and painted in their grandest manner. As they came in they took their seats and for a considerable time there was a profound silence — everyone was smoking, but not a word was spoken among them. At length one of the chiefs made a speech which was delivered to me by an interpreter and was as follows:

"My son, you are now flesh of our flesh and bone of our bone. By the ceremony which was performed this day, every drop of white blood was washed out of your veins. You are taken into the Caughnewaga nation and initiated into a war-like tribe. You are adopted into a great family and now received with great seriousness and solemnity in the room and place of a great man. After what has passed this day you are now one of us by an old strong law and custom. My son, you have now nothing to fear. We are now under the same obligations to love, support, and defend you that we are to love and to defend one another. Therefore you are to consider yourself as one of our people."

At this time I did not believe this fine speech, expecially that of the white blood being washed out

[15]Tinder.

of me; but since that time I have found that there was much sincerity in said speech: for from that day I never knew them to make any distinction between me and themselves in any respect whatever until I left them. If they had plenty of clothing, I had plenty; if we were scarce, we all shared one fate.

After this ceremony was over, I was introduced to my new kin and told that I was to attend a feast that evening, which I did. And as the custom was, they gave me also a bowl and wooden spoon which I carried with me to the place where there was a number of brass kettles full of boiled venison and green corn. Everyone advanced with his bowl and spoon and had his share given him. After this one of the chiefs made a short speech, and then we began to eat.

The name of one of the chiefs in this town was Tecanyaterighto, alias Pluggy,[16] and other Asal-lecosa, alias Mohawk Solomon. As Pluggy and his party were to start the next day to war to the frontiers of Virginia, the next thing to be performed was the war dance and their war songs. At their war dance they had both vocal and instrumental music. They had a short hollow gum [drum?], closed at one end with water in it, and parchment stretched over the open end thereof which they beat with one stick and made a sound nearly like a

[16] Pluggy was a Mingo, a name given to Senecas who had left the tribe in western New York and settled in Ohio. Later he had a village at modern Delaware, Ohio.

muffled drum. All those who were going on this expedition collected together and formed. An old Indian then began to sing and timed the music by beating on this drum, as the ancients formerly timed their music by beating the tabor.

On this the warriors began to advance, or move forward in concert, like well disciplined troops would march to the fife and drum. Each warrior had a tomahawk, spear, or war mallet in his hand, and they all moved regularly towards the east, or the way they intended to go to war. At length they all stretched their tomahawks toward the Potomac and giving a hideous shout or yell they wheeled quick about and danced in the same manner back. The next was the war song. In performing this, only one sang at a time, in a moving posture with a tomahawk in his hand, while all the other warriors were engaged in calling aloud, "*He-uh, he-uh*," which they constantly repeated while the war song was going on. When the warrior that was singing had ended his song, he struck a war-post with his tomahawk and with a loud voice told what warlike exploits he had done and what he now intended to do, which were answered by the other warriors with loud shouts of applause. Some who had not before intended to go to war at this time were so animated by this performance that they took up the tomahawk and sang the war song, which was answered with shouts of joy as they were then initiated into the present marching company.

The next morning this company all collected at one place with their heads and faces painted with various colors and packs upon their backs. They marched off all silent except the commander, who in the front sang the traveling song, which began in this manner: "*Hoo caughtainte heegama.*" Just as the rear passed the end of the town, they began to fire in their slow manner from the front to the rear, which was accompanied with shouts and yells from all quarters.

This evening I was invited to another sort of dance which was a kind of promiscuous dance. The young men stood in one rank, and the young women in another, about one rod apart, facing each other. The one that raised the tune or started the song held a small gourd or dry shell of a squash in his hand which contained beads or small stones that rattled. When he began to sing he timed the tune with his rattle. Both men and women danced and sang together, advancing towards each other, stooping until their heads would be touching together, and then ceased from dancing with loud shouts and retreated and formed again, and so repeated the same thing over and over for three or four hours without intermission. This exercise appeared to me at first irrational and insipid; but I found that in singing their tunes they used *ya ne no hoo wa ne* &c. like our *fa sol la*, and though they have no such thing as jingling verse yet they can intermix sentences with their notes and say what they please to each other and carry on the tune in concert. I found that this was a kind of wooing or courting dance, and as they advanced stooping with their heads together they could say what they pleased in each other's ear, without disconcerting their rough music, and the others or those near not hear what they said.

Shortly after this I went out to hunt in company with Mohawk Solomon, some of the Caughnewagas, and a Delaware Indian that was married to a Caughnewaga squaw. . . . When we returned to the town, Pluggy and his party had arrived and brought with them a considerable number of scalps and prisoners from the South Branch of the Potomac. They also brought with them an English Bible which they gave to a Dutch woman who was a prisoner, but as she could not read English she made a present of it to me, which was very acceptable.

I remained in this town until some time in October, when my adopted brother, called Tontileaugo, who had married a Wyandot squaw, took me with him to Lake Erie. We proceeded up the west branch of Muskingum and for some distance up the river the land was hilly, but intermixed with large bodies of tolerable rich upland and excellent bottoms. We proceeded on to the headwaters of the west branch of Muskingum . . . and from thence to the waters of Canesadooharie[17] there is a large body of rich, well-

[17] The Canesadooharie is the Huron River, which empties into Lake Erie about 10 miles east of Sandusky. It could be reached from the Mohican branch of the Walhonding River. There was at this time a Wyandot, or Huron, settlement at its mouth.

lying land—the timber is ash, walnut, sugar tree, buckeye, honey locust, and cherry, intermixed with some oak, hickory, &c. This tour was at the time that the black haws were ripe, and we were seldom out of sight of them; they were common here both in the bottoms and upland.

On this route we had no horses with us and when we started from the town, all the pack I carried was a pouch containing my books, a little dried venison, and my blanket. I had then no gun, but Tontileaugo, who was a first rate hunter, carried a rifle gun and every day killed deer, raccoons, or bears. We left the meat, excepting a little for present use, and carried the skins with us until we encamped and then stretched them with elm bark in a frame made with poles stuck in the ground and tied together with lynn or elm bark; and when the skins were dried by the fire, we packed them up and carried them with us the next day.

As Tontileaugo could not speak English, I had to make use of all the Caughnewaga I had learned, even to talk very imperfectly with him; but I found I learned to talk Indian faster this way than when I had those with me who could speak English.

As we proceeded down the Canesadooharie waters, our packs increased by the skins that were daily killed and became so very heavy that we could not march more than eight or ten miles per day. We came to Lake Erie about six miles west of the mouth of Canesadooharie. As the wind was very high the

evening we came to the lake, I was surprised to hear
the roaring of the water and see the high waves
that dashed against the shore like the ocean. We
encamped on a run near the lake and as the wind
fell that night, the next morning the lake was only in
a moderate motion, and we marched on the sand along
the side of the water, frequently resting ourselves as
we were heavily laden. I saw on the sand a number
of large fish that had been left in flat or hollow places;
as the wind fell and the waves abated, they were left
without water or only a small quantity, and numbers
of bald and gray eagles &c. were along the shore
devouring them.

Some time in the afternoon we came to a large
camp of Wyandots at the mouth of Canesadooharie,
where Tontileaugo's wife was. Here we were kindly
received: they gave us a kind of rough brown potatoes which grew spontaneously and were called by
the Caughewagas *ohnenata*. These potatoes, peeled
and dipped in raccoon's fat, taste nearly like our
sweet potatoes. They also gave us what they called
*caneheanta*, which is a kind of hominy made of green
corn, dried, and beans mixed together. . . .

We continued our camp at the mouth of Canesadooharie for some time, where we killed some deer
and a great many raccoons; the raccoons here were
remarkably large and fat. At length we all embarked
in a large birch bark canoe. This vessel was about
four feet wide and three feet deep, and about five and
thirty feet long; and though it could carry a heavy

burden it was so artfully and curiously constructed that four men could carry it several miles, or from one land place to another, or from the waters of the lake to the waters of the Ohio. We proceeded up Canesadooharie a few miles and went on shore to hunt; but to my great surprise they carried the vessel that we all came in up the bank and inverted it or turned the bottom up and converted it to a dwelling house, and kindled a fire before us to warm ourselves by and cook. With our baggage and ourselves in this house we were very much crowded, yet our little house turned off the rain very well.

We kept moving and hunting up this river until we came to the falls; here we remained some weeks and killed a number of deer, several bears, and a great many raccoons. From the mouth of this river to the falls is about five and twenty miles. On our passage up I was not much out from the river, but what I saw was good land and not hilly. About the falls is thin chestnut land, which is almost the only chestnut timber I ever saw in this country. . . .

As we had at this time no horses, everyone got a pack on his back and we steered an east course about twelve miles and encamped. The next morning we proceeded on the same course about ten miles to a large creek that empties into Lake Erie between Canesadooharie and Cuyahoga. Here they made their winter cabin in the following form: they cut logs about fifteen feet long and laid these logs upon each other and drove posts in the ground at each end to keep them together. The posts they tied together at the top with bark, and by this means raised a wall fifteen feet long and about four feet high and in the same manner they raised another wall opposite to this at about twelve feet distance. Then they drove forks in the ground in the center of each end and laid a strong pole from end on these forks; and from these walls to the poles they set up poles instead of rafters and on these they tied small poles in place of laths, and a cover was made of lynn bark which will run even in the winter season. . . .

At the end of these walls they set up split timber so that they had timber all round, excepting a door at each end. At the top in place of a chimney they left an open place, and for bedding they laid down the aforesaid kind of bark on which they spread bear skins. From end to end of this hut along the middle there were fires, which the squaws made of dry split wood, and the holes or open places that appeared the squaws stopped with moss which they collected from old logs; and at the door they hung a bearskin and notwithstanding the winters are hard here, our lodging was much better than what I expected.

It was some time in December [1755] when we got finished this winter cabin; but when we had got into this comparatively fine lodging another difficulty arose: we had nothing to eat. While I was traveling with Tontileaugo, as was before mentioned, and had plenty of fat venison, bear's meat, and raccoons, I then thought it was hard living without bread or salt; but now I began to conclude that if I had anything that would banish pinching hunger and keep soul and body together, I would be content.

While the hunters were all out exerting themselves to the utmost of their ability, the squaws and boys (in which class I was) were scattered out in the bottom hunting red haws, black haws, and hickory nuts. As it was too late in the year, we did not succeed in gathering haws; but we had tolerable success in scratching up hickory nuts from under a light snow which we carried with us lest the hunters should not succeed.

After our return the hunters came in who had killed only two small turkeys, which were but little among eight hunters and thirteen squaws, boys, and children; but they were divided with the greatest equity and justice. Everyone got their equal share. The next day the hunters turned out again and killed one deer and three bears. . . .

Some time in February the four warriors returned [they had gone out to steal horses] who had taken two scalps and six horses from the frontiers of Pennsylvania. The hunters could then scatter out a considerable distance from the winter cabin and encamp, kill meat, and bring it in upon horses; so that we commonly after this had plenty of provision.

In this month we began to make sugar. As some of the elm bark will strip at this season, the squaws after finding a tree that would do cut it down and with a crooked stick, broad and sharp at the end, took the bark off the tree and of this bark made vessels in a curious manner that would hold about two gallons each. They made above one hundred of these kind of vessels. In the sugar tree they cut a notch sloping down and at the end of the notch stuck in a tomahawk; in the place where they stuck the tomahawk they drove a long chip in order to carry the [sap] water out from the tree, and under this they set their vessel to receive it. As sugar trees were plenty and large here, they seldom or never notched a tree that was not two or three feet over.

They also made bark vessels for carrying the water that would hold about four gallons each. They had two brass kettles that held about fifteen gallons each and other smaller kettles in which they boiled the water. But as they could not at all times boil away the water as fast as it was collected, they made vessels of bark that would hold about one hundred gallons each for retaining the water; and though the sugar trees did not run every day, they had always a sufficient quantity of water to keep them boiling during the whole sugar season.

The way that we commonly used our sugar while encamped was by putting it in bear's fat until the fat was almost as sweet as the sugar itself, and in this we dipped our roasted venison. About this time some of the Indian lads and myself were employed in making and attending traps for catching raccoons, foxes, wildcats, &c. . . . .

About the latter end of March we began to prepare for moving into town in order to plant corn. The squaws were then frying the last of their bear's fat and making vessels to hold it; the vessels were made of deerskins which were skinned by pulling the skin off the neck without ripping. After they had taken off the hair they gathered it in small plaits round the neck and with a string drew it together like a purse. In the center a pin was put, below which they tied a string, and while it was wet they blew it up like a bladder and let it remain in this manner until it was dry, when it appeared nearly in the shape of a sugar loaf, but more rounding at the lower end. One of these vessels would hold about four or five gallons. In these vessels it was they carried their bear's oil.

When all things were ready we moved back to the falls of Canesadooharie. . . . On our arrival at the falls, as we had brought with us on horseback about two hundred weight of sugar, a large quantity of bear's oil, skins, &c., the canoe we had buried was not sufficient to carry all. Therefore we were obliged to make another one of elm bark. . . . We proceeded and arrived safe at Sunyendeand, which was a Wyandot town thay lay upon a small creek which empties into the little lake below the mouth of Sandusky.[18]

The town was about eighty rods above the mouth of the creek on the south side of a large plain, on which timber grew and nothing more but grass or

[18] Sunyendeand was a Wyandot, or Huron, town on the Sandusky River about five miles from its mouth.

nettles. In some places there were large flats where nothing but grass grew, about three feet high when grown, and in other places nothing but nettles, very rank, where the soil is extremely rich and loose. Here they planted corn. In this town there were also French traders who purchased our skins and furs, and we all got new clothes, paint, tobacco, &c.

After I had got my new clothes and my head done off like a red-headed woodpecker, I in company with a number of young Indians went down to the corn-field to see the squaws at work. When we came there they asked me to take a hoe, which I did and hoed for some time. The squaws applauded me as a good hand at the business; but when I returned to the town the old men hearing of what I had done chided me and said that I was adopted in the place of a great man and must not hoe corn like a squaw. They never had occasion to reprove me for anything like this again; as I never was extremely fond of work, I readily complied with their orders.

As the Indians on their return from their winter hunt bring in with them large quantities of bear's oil, sugar, dried venison, &c., at this time they have plenty and do not spare eating or giving. Thus they make away with their provision as quickly as possible. They have no such thing as regular meals: breakfast, dinner, or supper, but if anyone even the town folks would go to the same house several times in one day, he would be invited to eat of the best; and with them it is bad manners to refuse to eat when it is offered. If they will not eat, it is interpreted as a symptom of displeasure, or that the persons refusing to eat were angry with those who invited them. . . .

All the hunters and warriors continued in town about six weeks after we came in. They spent this time in painting, going from house to house, eating, smoking, and playing at a game resembling dice, or hustle cap.[19] They put a number of plum stones in a small bowl; one side of each stone is black and the other white. They then shake or hustle the bowl, calling, "*Hits, hits, hits, honesy, honesy, rago rago,*" which signifies calling for white or black, or what they wish to turn up. They then turn the bowl and count the whites and blacks. Some were beating their kind of drum and singing; others were employed in playing on a sort of flute, made of hollow cane; and others playing on the jew's-harp. Some part of this time was also taken up in attending the council house, where the chiefs and as many others as chose attended; and at night they were frequently employed in singing and dancing.

Towards the last of this time, which was in June 1756, they were all engaged in preparing to go to war against the frontiers of Virginia. When they were equipped, they went through their ceremonies, sang their war songs, &c. They all marched off, from fifteen to sixty years of age; and some boys only

[19] An old game, usually played with coins rather than the Indian's plum stones.

twelve years old were equipped with their bows and arrows and went to war; so that none were left in town but squaws and children, except myself, one very old man, and another about fifty years of age who was lame.

The Indians were then in great hopes that they would drive all the Virginians over the lake, which is all the name they know for the sea. They had some cause for this hope, because at this time the Americans were altogether unacquainted with war of any kind and consequently very unfit to stand their hand with such subtle enemies as the Indian were. The two old Indians asked me if I did not think that the Indians and French would subdue all America, except New England, which they said they had tried in old times. I told them I thought not. They said they had already drove them all out of the mountains and had chiefly laid waste the great valley between the North and South mountain from Potomac to James River, which is a considerable part of the best land in Virginia, Maryland, and Pennsylvania; and that the white people appeared to them like fools: they could neither guard against surprise, run, nor fight. These, they said, were their reason for saying that they would subdue the whites.

They asked me to offer my reasons for my opinion and told me to speak my mind freely. I told them that the white people to the east were very numerous, like the trees, and though they appeared to them to be fools, as they were not acquainted with their way of war, yet they were not fools. "Therefore, after some time they will learn your mode of war and turn upon you, or at least defend themselves." I found that the old men themselves did not believe they could conquer America, yet they were willing to propagate the idea in order to encourage the young men to go to war.

When the warriors left this town we had neither meat, sugar, nor bear's oil left. All that we had then to live on was corn pounded into coarse meal or small hominy. This they boiled in water, which appeared like well-thickened soup, without salt or anything else. For some time we had plenty of this kind of hominy; at length we were brought to very short allowance and as the warriors did not return as soon as they expected, we were in a starving condition and but one gun in town and very little ammunition. The old lame Wyandot concluded that he would go a hunting in a canoe and take me with him and try to kill deer in the water, as it was then watering time.

We went up Sandusky a few miles, then turned up a creek and encamped. We had lights prepared, as we were to hunt at night, and also a piece of bark and some bushes set up in the canoe in order to conceal ourselves from the deer. A little boy that was with us held the light, I worked the canoe, and the old man, who had his gun loaded with large shot when we came near the deer, fired and in this manner killed three deer in part of one night. We went to our fire, ate heartily, and in the morning returned to town in order to relieve the hungry and distressed. When we came to town the children were crying bitterly on account of pinching hunger. We delivered what we had taken and though it was little among so many, it was divided according to the strictest rules of justice.

We immediately set out for another hunt, but before we returned a part of the warriors had come in and brought with them on horseback a quantity of meat. These warriors had divided into different parties and all struck at different places in Augusta County [Virginia]. They brought in with them a considerable number of scalps, prisoners, horses, and other plunder. One of the parties brought in with them one Arthur Campbell, now Colonel Campbell who lives on Holston River near Royal Oak [Virginia]. As the Wyandots at Sunyendeand and those at Detroit were connected, Mr. Campbell was taken to Detroit; but he remained some time with me in this town. His company was very agreeable, and I was sorry when he left me. During his stay at Sunyendeand he borrowed my Bible and made some pertinent remarks on what he had read. One passage was where it is said, "It is good for man that he bear the yoke in his youth."[20] He said we ought to be resigned to the will of Providence, as we were now bearing the yoke in our youth. Mr. Campbell appeared to be then about sixteen or seventeen years of age.

[20] Lamentations: 3, 27.

There was a number of prisoners brought in by these parties, and when they were to run the gauntlet I went and told them how they were to act. One John Savage was brought in, a middle-aged man or about forty years old. He was to run the gauntlet. I told him what he had to do; and after this I fell into one of the ranks with the Indians, shouting and yelling like them; and as they were not very severe on him, as he passed me I hit him with a piece of pumpkin — which pleased the Indians much but hurt my feelings.

About the time that these warriors came in the green corn was beginning to be of use, so that we had either green corn or venison and sometimes both — which was comparatively high living. When we could have plenty of green corn, or roasting ears, the hunters became lazy and spent their time as already mentioned in singing and dancing, &c. They appeared to be fulfilling the Scriptures beyond those who profess to believe them in that of taking no thought of tomorrow; and also in living in love, peace, and friendship together without disputes. In this respect they shame those who profess Christianity.

In this manner we lived until October; then the geese, swans, ducks, cranes, &c. came from the north and alighted on this little lake without number, or innumerable. Sunyendeand is a remarkable place for fish in the spring and fowl both in the fall and spring. . . .

Some time in October another adopted brother, older than Tontileaugo, came to pay us a visit at

Sunyendeand and asked me to take a hunt with him on Cuyahoga. . . . I consulted with Tontileaugo on this occasion, and he told me that our old brother Tecaughretanego (which was his name) was a chief and a better man than he was, and if I went with him I might expect to be well used, but he said I might do as I pleased. . . .

I then went with Tecaughretanego to the mouth of the little lake where he met with the company he intended going with, which was composed of Caughnewagas and Ottawas. Here I was introduced to a Caughnewaga sister and others I had never before seen. My sister's name was Mary, which they pronounced *Maully.* I asked Tecaughretanego how it came that she had an English name? He said that he did not know that it was an English name, but it was the name the priest gave her when she was baptized, which he said was the name of the mother of Jesus. He said there were a great many of the Caughnewagas and Wyandots that were a kind of half-Roman Catholics; but as for himself he said that the priest and him could not agree, as they [the priests] held notions that contradicted both sense and reason and had the assurance to tell him that the book of God taught them these foolish absurdities; but he could not believe the great and good Spirit ever taught them any such nonsense and therefore he concluded that the Indian's old religion was better than this new way of worshipping God. . . [The hunting party went up the Cuyahoga and then moved overland southeastward about forty miles and camped on Beaver Creek for the winter. The principal prey was deer and beavers. Late in February the squaws began making maple sugar, and in March 1757 the party made its way back to the Cuyahoga River.]

I remember that Tecaughretanego, when something displeased him, said, "God damn it." I asked him if he knew what he then said? He said he did and mentioned one of their degrading expressions, which he supposed to be the meaning or something like the meaning of what he had said. I told him that it did not bear the least resemblance to it; that what he had said was calling upon the Great Spirit to punish the object he was displeased with. He stood for some time amazed and then said if this be the meaning of these words, what sort of people are the whites? When the traders were among us, these words seemed to be intermixed with all their discourse. He told me to reconsider what I had said, for he thought I must be mistaken in my definition. If I was not mistaken, he said, the traders applied these words not only wickedly but oftentimes very foolishly and contrary to sense or reason. He said he remembered once of a trader's accidentally breaking his gun-lock, and on that occasion calling out aloud, "God damn it." Surely, said he, the gun-lock was not an object worthy of punishment for *Owaneeyo*, or the Great Spirit. He also observed the traders often used this expression when they were in a good humor and not displeased with anything. I acknowledged that the traders used this expression very often in a

most irrational, inconsistent, and impious manner;
yet I still asserted that I had given the true meaning
of these words. He replied, "If so, the traders are
as bad as *Oonasahroona*," or the underground inhabitants, which is the name they give the devils, as they
entertain a notion that their place of residence is
under the earth.

We took up our birch bark canoes which we had
buried and found that they were not damaged by
the winter; but they not being sufficient to carry all
that we now had, we made a large chestnut bark
canoe, as elm bark was not to be found at this place.

We all embarked and had a very agreeable passage down the Cuyahoga and along the south side
of Lake Erie until we passed the mouth of Sandusky;
then the wind arose and we put in at the mouth
of the Miami of the Lake at Cedar Point,[21] where
we remained several days and killed a number of
turkeys, geese, ducks, and swans. The wind being
fair and the lake not extremely rough, we again
embarked, hoisted up sails, and arrived safe at the
Wyandot town nearly opposite to Fort Detroit, on
the north side of the river.[22]

[21] The Maumee River, which empties into Lake Erie
through Maumee Bay at Toledo.

[22] The Detroit River turns, and the French fort was on the
north side where the city now stands. Near it were three
Indian villages which Cadillac had induced the tribes to establish after he founded Detroit in 1701. Below the fort and
across the river was the Huron town. Above it was the
Ottawa town of Chief Pontiac. Opposite the Huron town was
a Potawatomi settlement, on the same side of the river as the
fort.

Here we found a number of French traders, every one very willing to deal with us for our beaver. We bought ourselves fine clothes, ammunition, paint, tobacco, &c., and according to promise they purchased me a new gun. Yet we had parted with only about one-third of our beaver. At length a trader came to town with French brandy. We purchased a keg of it and held a council about who was to get drunk and who was to keep sober. I was invited to get drunk, but I refused the proposal. Then they told me that I must be one of those who were to take care of the drunken people. I did not like this, but of two evils I chose that which I thought was the least and fell in with those who were to conceal the arms and keep every dangerous weapon we could out of their way and endeavor, if possible, to keep the drinking club from killing each other, which was a very hard task. Several times we hazarded our own lives and got ourselves hurt in preventing them from slaying each other. Before they had finished this keg, near one-third of the town was introduced to this drinking club; they could not pay their part, as they had already disposed of all their skins, but that made no odds. All were welcome to drink.

When they were done with this keg, they applied to the traders and procured a kettle full of brandy at a time, which they divided out with a large wooden spoon — and so they went on and never quit while they had a single beaver skin. When the trader had got all our beaver, he moved off to the Ottawa town, about a mile above the Wyandot town.

When the brandy was gone and the drinking club sober, they appeared much dejected. Some of them were crippled, others badly wounded, a number of their fine new shirts torn, and several blankets were burned. A number of squaws were also in this club and neglected their corn planting. We could now hear the effects of the brandy in the Ottawa town. . . .

About the middle of June the Indians were almost all gone to war, from sixteen to sixty; yet Tecaughretanego remained in town with me. Though he had formerly, when they were at war with the southern nations, been a great warrior and an eminent councilor, and I think as clear and able a reasoner upon any subject that he had an opportunity of being acquainted with as I ever knew, yet he had all along been against this war and had strenuously opposed it in council. He said if the English and French had a quarrel, let them fight their own battles themselves; it is not our business to intermediate therewith.

Before the warriors returned we were very scarce of provision and though we did not commonly steal from one another yet we stole during this time anything that we could eat from the French, under the notion that it was just for us to do so because they supported their soldiers, and our squaws, old men, and children were suffering on account of the war as our hunters were all gone.

Sometime in August the warriors returned and brought in with them a great many scalps, prisoners, horses, and plunder; and the common report among the young warriors was that they would entirely subdue *Tulhasaga*, that is, the English, or it might be literally rendered the Morning Light inhabitants.

About the first of November a number of families were preparing to go on their winter hunt, and all agreed to cross the lake together. We encamped at the mouth of the [Detroit] River the first night, and a council was held whether we should cross through by the three islands[23] or coast it round [the west end of] the lake . . . We concluded to coast it round the lake and in two days we came to the mouth of the Miami of the Lake and landed on Cedar Point, where we remained several days. Here we held a council and concluded we would take a driving hunt in concert and in partnership.

The river in this place is about a mile broad, and as it and the lake form a kind of neck, which terminates in a point, all the hunters (which were fifty-three) went up the river and we scattered ourselves from the river to the lake. When we first began to move we were not in sight of each other, but as we all raised the yell we could move regularly together by the noise. At length we came in sight of each other and appeared to be marching in good order. Before we came to the point both the squaws and boys in the canoes were scattered up the river and along the lake to prevent the deer from making their escape by water. As we advanced near the point

[23]The several islands north of Sandusky Bay included North, Middle, and South Bass islands and the much larger Pelée and Kelley's islands.

the guns began to crack slowly; and after some time the firing was like a little engagement. The squaws and boys were busy tomahawking the deer in the water, and we shooting them down on the land. We killed in all about thirty deer, though a great many made their escape by water. We had now great feasting and rejoicing, as we had plenty of hominy, venison, and wild fowl. . . . As cold weather was now approaching we began to feel the doleful effects of extravagantly and foolishly spending the large quantity of beaver we had taken in our last winter's hunt. We were all nearly in the same circumstances — scarcely one had a shirt to his back, but each of us had an old blanket which we belted round us in the day and slept in at night, with a deer or bearskin under us for our bed. . . .

[Smith's party began the winter hunt in the region between the Sandusky and Scioto rivers and then settled on Olentangy Creek. In February 1758 hunting was so unproductive that he, an older warrior, and an Indian boy endured several days of great hunger. His elder "brother," Tecaughretanego, who was too lame to hunt, sought to reassure him.]

He then said he had something of importance to tell me, if I was now composed and ready to hear it. I told him that I was ready to hear him. He said the reason why he deferred his speech till now was because few men are in a right humor to hear good talk when they are extremely hungry, as they are then generally fretful and discomposed, "but as you appear now to enjoy calmness and serenity of mind, I will now communicate to you the thoughts of my heart and those things that I know to be true.

"Brother, as you have lived with the white people you have not had the same advantage of knowing that the Great Being above feeds his people and gives them their meat in due season, as we Indians have who are frequently out of provisions and yet are wonderfully supplied, and that so frequently that it is evidently the hand of the great *Owaneeyo* that does this. Whereas the white people have commonly large stocks of tame cattle that they can kill when they please, and also their barns and cribs filled with grain and therefore have not the same opportunity of seeing and knowing that they are supported by the Ruler of Heaven and earth.

"Brother, I know that you are now afraid that we will all perish with hunger, but you have no just reason to fear this.

"Brother, I have been young but am now old. I have been frequently under the like circumstances that we now are, and that sometime or other in almost every year of my life; yet I have hitherto been supported and my wants supplied in time of need.

"Brother, *Owaneeyo* sometimes suffers us to be in want in order to teach us our dependence upon Him and to let us know that we are to love and serve Him; and likewise to know the worth of the favors that we receive and to make us more thankful.

"Brother, be assured that you will be supplied with food and that just in the right time; but you must continue diligent in the use of means: go to sleep and rise early in the morning and go a hunting; be strong and exert yourself like a man, and the Great Spirit will direct your way."

The next morning I went out and steered about an east course. I proceeded on slowly for about five miles and saw deer frequently; but as the crust on the snow made a great noise they were always running before I spied them so that I could not get a shot. A violent appetite returned and I became intolerably hungry. It was now that I concluded I would run off to Pennsylvania, my native country. As the snow was on the ground and Indian hunters almost the whole of the way before me, I had but a poor prospect of making my escape, but my case appeared desperate. If I stayed here I thought I would perish with hunger, and if I met with Indians they could but kill me.

I then proceeded on as fast as I could walk, and when I got about ten or twelve miles from our hut I came upon fresh buffalo tracks. I pursued after and in a short time came in sight of them as they were passing through a small glade. I ran with all my might and headed them, where I lay in ambush and killed a very large cow. I immediately kindled a fire and began to roast meat, but could not wait till it was done; I ate it almost raw. When hunger was abated, I began to be tenderly concerned for my old

Indian brother and the little boy I had left in a perishing condition. I made haste and packed up what meat I could carry, secured what I left from the wolves, and returned homewards.

I scarcely thought on the old man's speech while I was almost distracted with hunger, but on my return was much affected with it, reflected on myself for my hard-heartedness and ingratitude in attempting to run off and leave the venerable old man and little boy to perish with hunger. I also considered how remarkably the old man's speech had been verified in our providentially obtaining a supply. I thought also of that part of his speech which treated of the fractious dispositions of hungry people, which was the only excuse I had for my base inhumanity in attempting to leave them in the most deplorable situation. . . .

We remained here until some time in April 1758. At this time Tecaughretanego had recovered so that he could walk about. . . . When we came to the little lake at the mouth of Sandusky, we called at the Wyandot town. Here we diverted ourselves several days by catching rock fish in a small creek, the name of which is also Sunyendeand, which signifies rock fish. They fished in the night with lights and struck the fish with gigs or spears. The rock fish here when they begin first to run up the creek to spawn are exceedingly fat, sufficient to fry themselves. . . .

Shortly after this we left Sunyendeand and in three days arrived at Detroit, where we remained this summer. Some time in May we heard that General Forbes, with seven thousand men, was preparing to carry on a campaign against Fort Duquesne, which then stood near where Fort Pitt was afterwards erected.[24] Upon receiving this news a number of runners were sent off by the French commander at Detroit to urge the different tribes of Indian warriors to repair to Fort Duquesne.

Some time in July 1758 the Ottawas, Ojibwas,[25] Potawatomies, and Wyandots rendezvoused at Detroit to prepare for the encounter of General Forbes. The common report was that they would serve him as they did General Braddock and obtain much plunder. From this time until fall we had frequent accounts of Forbes's army by Indian runners that were sent out to watch their motion. They espied them frequently from the mountains ever after they left Fort Loudon.

Notwithstanding their vigilance, Colonel [James] Grant with his Highlanders stole a march upon them and in the night took possession of a hill about eighty rods from Fort Duquesne. This hill is on that account called Grant's Hill to this day. The French and Indians knew not that Grant and his men were

[24] Brigadier John Forbes was leading 6700 men across Pennsylvania to capture Fort Duquesne, cutting a new road as he marched. He finally succeeded in driving out the French and seizing a burned and empty fort on Nov. 25, 1758.

[25] The Ojibwas were better known as the Chippewas. Their principal villages at this time were at Saginaw Bay and on the Straits of Mackinac; others were in the Lake Superior region.

there until they beat the drum and played upon the bagpipe just at daylight. They then flew to arms, and the Indians ran up under cover of the banks of the Allegheny and Monongahela for some distance and then sallied out from the banks of the rivers and took possession of the hill above Grant; and as he was on the point of it in sight of the fort, they immediately surrounded him, and as he had his Highlanders in ranks and in very close order, and the Indians scattered and concealed behind trees, they defeated him with the loss only of a few warriors. Most of the Highlanders were killed or taken prisoners.[26]

After this defeat the Indians held a council but were divided in their opinions. Some said that General Forbes would now turn back and go home the way he came, as Dunbar had done when General Braddock was defeated; others supposed he would come on. The French urged the Indians to stay and see the event; but as it was hard for the Indians to be absent from their squaws and children at this season of the year, a great many of them returned home to their hunting. After this the remainder of the Indians, some French regulars, and a number of Canadians marched off in quest of General Forbes. They

[26]This brief account of Col. Grant's attack is basically correct. With 840 men he moved ahead of Forbes' main body and got within sight of Fort Duquesne on Sept. 14 undetected. Then he unaccountably threw away his surprise and with bagpipes tootling and drums beating he marched his troops in formation down the hill—to defeat. He lost 315 men in killed or captured and he himself was made prisoner.

met his army near Fort Ligonier and attacked them, but were frustrated in their design. They said that Forbes's men were beginning to learn the art of war, and that there were a great number of American riflemen along with the redcoats who scattered out, took trees, and were good marksmen. Therefore they found they could not accomplish their design and were obliged to retreat.

When they returned from the battle to Fort Duquesne, the Indians concluded that they would go to their hunting. The French endeavored to persuade them to stay and try another battle. The Indians said if it was only the redcoats they had to do with, they could soon subdue them, but they could not withstand *Ashalecoa*, or the Great Knife, which was the name they gave the Virginians. They then returned home to their hunting, and the French evacuated the fort, which General Forbes came and took possession of without further opposition late in the year 1758 and at this time began to build Fort Pitt.

When Tecaughretanego had heard the particulars of Grant's defeat, he said that he could not well account for his contradictory and inconsistent conduct. He said as the art of war consists in ambushing and surprising our enemies and in preventing them from ambushing and surprising us, Grant in the first place acted like a wise and experienced warrior in artfully approaching in the night without being discovered; but when he came to the place and the Indians were lying asleep outside of the fort, between him and the Allegheny River, in place of slipping up quietly and falling upon them with their broadswords, they beat the drums and played upon the bagpipes. He said he could account for this inconsistent conduct no other way than by supposing that he had made too free with spirituous liquors during the night and became intoxicated about daylight.

But to return. This year we hunted up Sandusky and down Scioto and took nearly the same route that we had done the last hunting season. We had considerable success and returned to Detroit some time in April 1759.

Shortly after this Tecaughretanego, his son Nungany, and myself went from Detroit (in an elm bark canoe) to Caughnewaga, a very ancient Indian town about nine miles above Montreal, where I remained until about the first of July. I then heard of a French ship at Montreal that had English prisoners on board in order to carry them overseas and exchange them. I went privately off from the Indians and got also on board; but as General Wolfe[27] had stopped the River St. Lawrence, we were all sent to prison in Montreal, where I remained four months. Some time in November we were all sent off from this place to Crown Point[28] and exchanged.

[27] Major General James Wolfe besieged Quebec in the summer of 1759 and captured it on Sept. 13. The French provincial government fled up river to Montreal, which was not surrendered until a year later.

[28] Crown Point on Lake Champlain had just been abandoned by the French and taken over by the English.

Early in the year 1760 I came home to Conococheague and found that my people could never ascertain whether I was killed or taken until my return. They received me with great joy, but were surprised to see me so much like an Indian both in my gait and gesture. Upon inquiry I found that my sweetheart was married a few days before I arrived. My feelings I must leave on this occasion for those of my readers to judge who have felt the pangs of disappointed love, as it is impossible now for me to describe the emotion of soul I felt at that time. . . .

# 4

## Cleaveland's Letters and Diary

*

### *A Chaplain at Ticonderoga*
1758

# A Chaplain at Ticonderoga
## 1758

*The summer of 1758 marked the end of the third year of the French and Indian War in America. So far the French had enjoyed the best of it. The English attempt to sieze Fort Duquesne (Pittsburgh) in 1755 had met decisive defeat. The next year saw the destruction of Fort Oswego on Lake Ontario, while Lord Loudoun laid plans to invade Canada. In 1757 he went up against the fortress at Louisbourg and failed miserably. In his absence Fort William Henry on Lake George was taken by Montcalm and razed, while another French and Indian detachment burned out a German settlement on the Mohawk River.*

*Now in 1758 the combined British and provincial forces were under the interim command of Major General James Abercromby, who planned to take the new French fort at Ticonderoga on Lake Champlain as the first step in a new invasion of Canada. His task force for this objective seemed overwhelming: 6500 regulars made up of seven regiments and a battalion of the Royal Artillery plus 9500 provincials consisting of six regiments from Massachusetts, four from Connecticut, one each from New*

*York, Rhode Island, and New Jersey, Major Rogers'
Rangers, Col. Bradstreet's boatmen, and some
Mohawk Indians under Sir William Johnson—
16,000 men in all. All during May and June these
units swept through Albany and pushed up to the
head of Lake George, where another Fort William
Henry would rise.*

*Within Fort Carillon at Ticonderoga, General
Montcalm had only about 3500 French regulars
and Canadian militia, far more than the masonry
fort could hold, so that most of the troops camped
around it. He set them to work digging entrenchments across the peninsula before the fort and felling
trees to form a barrier in front of the trenches. This
entanglement of branches rose more than six feet
high and was a hundred yards in depth. At the same
time Montcalm made preparations to abandon the
fort and retreat to his second fort at Crown Point.*

*The Anglo-American army embarked on Lake
George in the early morning of July 4. Red, blue,
and green uniforms, tan buckskins, and Scotch
plaids were patches of color among more than a
thousand batteaux and whaleboats that covered the
width of the lake. Great rafts conveyed the black
cannon. The sun flashed on muskets, swords, band
instruments, and glistening Indian skins. The spec-
tacle of this huge, water borne army was as colorful
as anything seen in the war, and even the participants were impressed as they looked around.*

*After they landed in a cove, an advance force under Col. Lord Howe, second in command, plunged into the woods toward the fort. Unexpectedly it collided with a French reconnaissance force and routed it, killing a hundred and seizing about 150 prisoners. But in the clash the British suffered 230 wounded and 87 killed — among them the popular and spirited Lord Howe. The whole dash of the enterprise was punctured by his death, but Abercromby pushed his men closer to the fort next day. The French prisoners declared that Montcalm had 6000 men and was expecting a heavy reinforcement. Abercromby believed them and decided he must attack without waiting for his cannon to be rolled up.*

*The assault began next day about noon with the regulars leading, supported by the Massachusetts regiments. The rest were held in reserve. Wave after wave of redcoats threw themselves against the barrier of trees and were shot down by an enemy they could not see. Fires were started among the green branches but were put out by the French. At 7 P.M. the sixth and last charge was finally halted, and withdrawal to the landing place began. More than 1600 casualties had been suffered. The sudden retreat revealed as poor judgment as the attack. The French could not believe their luck and credited it to Divine favor.*

*How did all these preparations, this stupendous advance over the water, the furious attack and retreat appear to an American participant? We have the account of a Massachusetts chaplain who kept a diary and wrote regularly to his wife. He witnessed as well as any single individual could the exciting and tragic events of that campaign, and relates them better than most participants could. John Cleaveland was born in Connecticut in 1722 and entered Yale in 1741 to prepare for the ministry. At the end of his junior year his family was swept up in the religious revival called the Great Awakening, which appealed to the emotions rather than the intellect, questioned the necessity of an educated clergy, and aroused the fervor of contrite sinners. Staid congregations split into New Lights and Old Lights. As a consequence, young Cleaveland was not allowed to finish his senior year at Yale. Instead he studied theology with a New Light or evangelical pastor in another town and then supplied a New Light church in Boston.*

*North of Boston the Congregational Church in Chebacco (now Essex) had split, and the New Light group called him to become pastor in December 1746. He was ordained the next year and was married to Mary Dodge of Ipswich. They eventually had seven children. Cleaveland remained at Chebacco the rest of his life, uniting the split church in 1774. He died in 1799 at the age of 77.*

*In March 1758 Governor Thomas Pownall commissioned him as chaplain to the 3rd Massachusetts regiment under Col. Jonathan Bagley. He participated in the Ticonderoga campaign, as related here, and returned home at the end of October. The next year he accompanied the regiment to garrison Louisbourg (captured at last) on Cape Breton Island. In 1775 and 1776 he served as chaplain again, and all his four sons were in the Revolutionary army too.*

*His diary and his letters were seen and copied by Peter Force, possibly in the 1840's, for his great historical publishing project. All of Force's papers went to the Library of Congress. Excerpts from the diary were published in the* Historical Collections *of the Essex Institute in 1874–75. The original Cleaveland diary was given, appropriately enough, to the library of the restored Fort Ticonderoga, which published it in its* Bulletin *in 1959 and by whose kind permission we offer part of it. The originals of Cleaveland's letters are not known, but the Library of Congress has permitted publication of its Force transcripts. We have interspersed them among the diary entries to make as full a narrative as possible. The reader may be surprised at how religious the provincials were, and how they viewed themselves as serving almost on a crusade.*

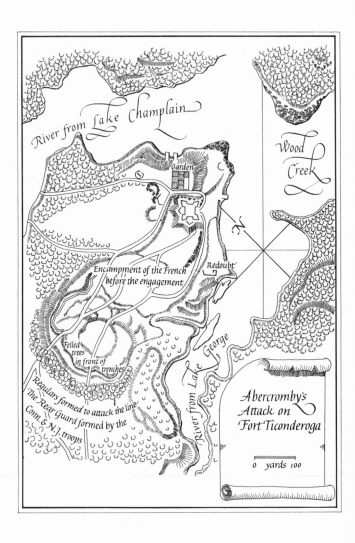

River from Lake Champlain

Wood Creek

Garden

Encampment of the French
before the engagement

Redoubt

Felled
trees
in front of
trenches

Regulars formed to attack the line
The Rear Guard formed by the
Conn. & N.J. troops

River from Lake George

Abercromby's
Attack on
Fort Ticonderoga

0   yards  100

# Cleaveland's Letters and Diary

*Flat Bush, about five miles above Albany
at Capt. Van Buren's,[1] June 10, 1758*

*My dear and loving wife,*

We arrived at this place last night; we have had a very tedious rout thro' unknown ways; Col. Bagley is not arrived yet with his regiment. I left Boston the Thursday after I went from home, and by reason of the rain we got no farther than Spencer, about fifteen miles west of Worcester, where we kept the Sabbath with Mr. Eaton, an eminent servant of Christ, where Brother preached in the forenoon and I preached in the afternoon, and just as we were going into the meeting house in the afternoon, Col. Bagley came up and stopped till the exercise was over and then went to Brookfield, where we overtook him the next morning, and after we rode with him about three miles we parted. He went after his regiment that were gone to Northampton, and we went to Springfield to go the old road, and on the bounds of Sheffield we came across the Connecticut forces, among which was Brother Aaron. My company were Brother Ebenezer Cleaveland and Dr. Rea.[2]

[1] Capt. Van Buren apparently was a veteran who ran an inn or tavern in Flat Bush and gave special attention to the needs of officers stationed in the vicinity.

[2] Dr. Caleb Rea was surgeon to Col. Bagley's regiment.

I have been in very good health ever since I came from home, tho' much fatigued by riding a very dull horse. How it is with our Chebacco people in the army I can't tell, as I have not seen Col. Bagley's regiment, they being yet in the woods, except some who belong to Col. [Ebenezer] Nichols' viz. Ensign Giddings and [Lieut.] Jonathan Burnham, and they are well and indeed as to those that are here perhaps there was never such a number together so healthy as they be at present and in high spirits, officers and soldiers, to go forward to do business.

The General Abercrombie and Lord Howe are gone before to the lakes, and we expect to be marching after in a day or two. If God be for us we shall have success. The regiments, as I marched after them, behaved exceedingly civilly through the country, except Marblehead company, which behaved extremely bad and have the curse of the country wished upon them.

I don't forget you, my family and people, nor do I think that you or they will forget me or the army. Prayer will do great things. I hope and pray that God may be with you and them that are at home, and us that are in the army. I doubt not that I shall see you thro' Divine Goodness. As Col. Bagley is not arrived with his regiment and Col. Ruggles' chaplain is not come, I perform the duty of chaplain to Col. Ruggles'[3] regiment at his desire.

[3]Timothy Ruggles became a Loyalist in the Revolution and died in 1798.

New York and New Jersey forces are gone to Fort Edward. The woods swarm with locusts here which make such a noise as is enough to dull one's senses. I conclude (praying that God would be with you, the children, my family and people)

*Your affectionate husband,*

John Cleaveland

P.S. *June 12.* We are still at Flat Bush at Capt. Van Buren's and when we shall go from hence we know not, Col. Bagley not being arrived here as yet, neither have I heard from him since I left him. Two French deserters are come into Fort Edward a few days ago and report that the French in their fort are extremely distressed for want of provision that they have sent seven or eight thousand men to Cape Breton, not having heard till a few days ago that we were coming against them this way with an army of twenty thousand men. I have something of a cold at present, but hope it is going off.

*I am yours &c*

J. C.

*June 15, 1758, Thursday.* Last night Capt. Goodwin arrived here who parted with us when we parted with Col. Bagley at Brookfield and informs me that Col. Bagley is arrived at Green Bush[4] with his regiment and may be expected at Flat Bush today. I want to be moving forward. Two or three in both

[4]Green Bush was across the Hudson from Albany.

Col. Ruggles' and Col. Nichols' regiments after being
here but five or six days were taken sick and left so
by the regiments, and I fear very much that the
smallpox will get into the army, so many of the army
both officers and soldiers daily going into the city.
About four o'clock this day Col. Bagley's regiment
began to come into Flat Bush. All [of] Capt. [Ste-
phen] Whipple's company arrived safe except one
Jacob Laskin, whom they left at Northampton or
Hadley much indisposed by an unlucky blow upon
his blind eye. Prayed with three or four companies
of our regiment this evening. I was much pleased
to meet my friends of Chebacco.

*16, Friday.* This morning attended prayers with
several companies of my regiment. There happened
a sad affair in our regiment. Several persons of Capt.
[Ebenezer] Morrow's company were put under guard
for killing some of our landlord's cattle, fresh meat
being found upon them.

*17, Saturday.* Attended prayers. Lt. Col. Whitcomb[5] was present, this was the first time. This day
came on the courtmartial for the trial of those above
mentioned, and they found three guilty who were
condemned to be whipped: two fifty lashes and one
twenty-five, but one was discharged by the colonel
and the other two received but 10 lashes apiece: viz.
Retire Bacon and Joseph Brown.

[5] John Whitcomb became a major general of militia in the
Revolution and died in 1812.

*Flat Bush, five miles above Albany,*
*June 17, 1758*

*My dear and loving wife,*

I have just a minute to write to let you know that I am well in health, for which I bless God and hope these will find you in good health and the family. I am now at Capt. Van Buren's where I have been a week last night, waiting for our regiment, which arrived here but the day before yesterday in very good health, and all arrived except Jacob Laskin, whom they left at Hadley or Northampton (having received an unlucky blow upon his lame eye) under the care of a doctor there. We expect to march from here toward Fort Edward Monday next . . .

*19, Monday.* Prayers early because of our marching towards Schenectady.[6] Settled my account with Capt. Van Buren which amounted to a dollar and a half besides the dollar Col. Ruggles paid for me; and then passed the river and the whole regiment marched and arrived safe at night to Schenectady and put up at Mr. Nicholas Van Patten's, Col. Whitcomb, Dr. Rea, Capt. [Andrew] Giddings and I having marched full 19 or 20 English miles. The doctor and I rode on horseback, having providentially found them; they had been missing several days and been sought after to no effect. I acknowl-

[6]Obviously there had been a change in orders, for Cleaveland had told his wife he expected to go north to Fort Edward, not west to Schenectady and the German Flats, a settlement of Palatine immigrants on the Mohawk River, where Herkimer now stands.

edge God in this thing and adore him for all his goodness to me since I've been in this campaign and pray that He would be with me and the army and the several regiments destined to German Flats. My regiment don't seem to be well pleased with our going to that place, but would rather have gone to Crown Point and Quebec.

20, *Tuesday*. This day tarried at Schenectady, took some view of the town, which is very pleasantly and compactly situated; according to my judgement it is as large as Charleston, near Boston.[7] They have a stone church or meeting house, the minister is a Dutchman and so are the generality of the people. The regiment was this evening called together for prayers; this was in fact the first time that Col. Bagley has had an opportunity of attending prayers since I have been with the regiment, who has given orders to the captains to attend every day while we tarry here at six o'clock in the morning and seven in the evening. After prayers Major [Joseph] Ingersoll came to town from Albany and brings word that they had advice there that Major Rogers[8] had been out with a party of fifty men somewhere [on] the lake and had an engagement with the enemy in which he lost six men and received a slight wound himself

[7] In his next letter to his wife Cleaveland said Schenectady was as large as Salem.

[8] Robert Rogers commanded the Rangers, a scouting and raiding force for Gen. Abercromby. His exploits against the French and Indians were fast making him legendary. See the next narrative for one of them.

in one of his legs. There was also this day an alarming rumor in this town that Fort Edward was besieged by the enemy, and many of the officers supposed that they heard the report of great guns from that way in their march to this [place] on Monday till night, and some asserted that they heard them this morning, but those that arrived here this evening from Albany heard nothing of it there.

*21, Wednesday.* This morning attended prayers at six o'clock. The regiment still remains in good health, excepting some few particulars, none sick with a fever for which I bless God. I pray God to be with us to keep us from sin, sickness and every evil occurrence, that He would be with wife, family and people, be their God, strength and everlasting portion. After prayers and breakfast we hired a room for the 3rd officers' staff officers to cook their victuals in and were to give 20 shillings York currency a week rent. This evening prayers were omitted by reason of a shower of rain and now we are just informed from Albany that Rogers has lost but four men and is gone out again with three hundred men in great wrath against the enemy.

*22, Thursday.* Last night quite late arrived orders from General Stanwix [9] for the two companies of Col.

[9] Brigadier John Stanwix (1690?–1766) was building Fort Stanwix at the east end of Lake Oneida to protect the Mohawk River settlements from French raids coming out of the west.

Whiting[10] that are in town and for one company and half of another in our regiment to march directly to Half Moon;[11] it is certified that a flag of truce is come into Fort Edward. We attended prayers and then supped at our new lodgings, having dined with Domine Vroman, the Dutch minister in Schenectady.

*23, Friday.* Prayers late this morning by reason of a shower. This evening Col. Bagley received orders immediately to march toward Fort Edward upon the arrival of Col. Joseph Williams' [Massachusetts] regiment to Schenectady, eight companies of which are to be stationed in this town. The officers and soldiers seem pleased with a thought of joining the army; the Lord God be with us in all our marches and engagements.

*24, Saturday.* This morning I gave a short word of exhortation to the soldiers, as we are in some expectation to march this day, and Mr. Johnson of Garrit Brook, about ten miles to the southwest of this town, being present prayed with the regiment, and after prayers a most melancholy accident: as one of the soldiers was exercising in the Prussian way, when he came to fire, not considering that his gun was

[10] Col. Nathaniel Whiting (1724–1771), a Yale graduate, commanded the 2nd Connecticut regiment.

[11] Half Moon was on the west bank of the Hudson, 13 miles north of Albany where the Mohawk River empties into the Hudson.

charged, it went off with two balls, one went through a soldier sitting at a small distance, entering a little below his right shoulder and coming out by his left breast. His name is Moody of Haverhill, who died about two hours after. The other ball struck another man's leg, hit the bone and glanced out the same side. His name is [Enoch] Marsh, also of Haverhill, and a third man had one of the balls pass through his jacket and shirt and just touched the end of his finger. He narrowly escaped with his life and received no hurt.

This night Elisha Moody, the man killed with the ball, was buried. A great part of the regiment attended, and the company under arms that he belonged to. After he was let down into the grave I prayed and then made a speech to the soldiers. A court of inquiry was made upon the man, William Herrick, that fired the gun which did such mischief, and he was cleared; the poor fellow is much cast down!

At prayers this evening I made a speech of some length to the regiment, as they were to march the next day early. There were present many of the town's people, both men and women. The people of the town are very sorry that we must march from them. The people in Schenectady were quite a civil people and they have quite a good sort of a man to their minister.

25, *Sabbath.* This morning after prayers we set out for Half Moon and arrived there at about sun setting, a march of the best part of twenty miles. I cautioned the regiment in the morning to remember the Sabbath day to keep it holy, and they did behave quite civilly in general, but I never saw just such a Sabbath before . . . At Half Moon we found two Connecticut regiments, Col. Lyman's[12] and Wooster's.[13] This night we encamped on the hard floor with a blanket under us and another upon us.

*June 26, 1758, at Half Moon*
*My dear and loving wife,*

This is the third time of my writing to you since I came into these parts, and I was in hopes of hearing from you before this time. I greatly long to hear from you and my dear family. I am at present and have been for some time in as good health as I have been for this twelvemonth past. I pray God to continue it and that you and the little ones may constantly be favored with the same blessing.

[The second paragraph relates the musket accident and the march to Half Moon.]

We are bound now to the lake as fast as we can get along, Col. Williams of Roxbury with his regi-

[12] Phineas Lyman (1715–1774) commanded the 1st Connecticut regiment and led one column toward Ticonderoga when Lord Howe led the other.
[13] David Wooster (1711–1777) was a Yale classmate of Lyman and commanded the 4th Connecticut regiment. As a major general in the Revolution he was killed in action.

ment having gone to take our place at Schenectady and should have marched this day but are hindered by the rain. We expect to be at the lake this week. We hear that the general is moving from Fort Edward to the lake. The troops seem to be exceedingly engaged to go forward: the Lord give them wisdom and courage, success and victory. I expect that within three weeks from this time we shall see the strength of Canada at the lake, somewhere near Ticonderoga. Doubtless then many must change worlds; the Lord prepare all for it that must take their leave of time then, and I hope you will pray for me.

I don't forget you nor my little ones, nor the people of my charge. Chebacco people in Capt. Whipple's company are all well that are here. Brother Ebenezer Cleaveland has gone along up to the lake with Col. Preble[14] as chaplain of his regiment. I have not seen him since Col. Preble engaged him to go with him. There are some excellent men in this army, and some excellent chaplains. I hope God designs good for our land yet, but we must not trust in an arm of flesh. God may blast us a thousand ways. I fear the smallpox will spread in the army. One of our regiment broke out with it last night. He got it, I suppose, of some market woman who came to Flat Bush at Capt. Van Buren's to sell cake.

---

[14]Col. Jedediah Preble commanded a Massachusetts regiment, became a brigadier general of militia in the Revolution, and died in 1784. He was the father of Commodore Edward Preble.

I wish you the best of Heaven's blessings and pray God we may see one another again under the smiles of Heaven. Give my love to all my people and neighbors and inquiring friends and your mother whom I daily think on.

*I subscribe yours affectionately,*
John Cleaveland

27, *Tuesday*. This morning Mr. Ingersoll, Col. Wooster's chaplain, prayed with our regiment, and we set out and arrived at Stillwater[15] about one o'clock, where we overtook Col. Wooster's regiment and dined with the colonel in the fort, and then he marched forward and our regiment, after refreshing themselves, marched also forward. But the field officers tarried at Stillwater and lodged in the fort.

28, *Wednesday*. Marched from Stillwater to Saratoga Fort, where we put up and tarried all night. Fourteen miles from Stillwater to Saratoga.

29, *Thursday*. Marched from Saratoga to Fort Miller 5 miles and from thence to Fort Edward 7 miles and put up and tarried all night.[16] Lodged in Commissary Tucker's tent and fared well.

[15] Stillwater fort was on the west bank of the Hudson about 10 miles above Half Moon.
[16] Fort Edward, on the east bank of Hudson, was erected in 1755. Today's town carries the same name.

*30, Friday.* This day tarried at Fort Edward. One company of a hundred men under Capt. Morrow were draughted out of the regiment to tarry at Fort Edward.

*July 1st.* This day being Saturday, after sending my horse by Isaac Haskill to Capt. Van Buren's with the following articles, viz. bridle, saddle, boots, spurs, one pair of yarn stockings, and one pair of double-soled German pumps, set out on foot to Lake George. Dined at Halfway Brook with Col. Nichols, Col. Cummings, and Mr. Morrill, the chaplain, and set out again. Arrived at the Lake before sunset, something fatigued, and lodged with Mr. Forbush, chaplain to Col. Ruggles.

*2, Sabbath.* This day joined regiments with Col. Ruggles for public worship. Mr. Forbush preached in the forenoon from Exodus 17 upon Moses sending Joshua to fight against Amalek while he with the rod of God in his hand went upon the top of the hill with Aaron and Hur, and an excellent sermon he preached, well adapted to the occasion. Afternoon I preached to a large concourse from Ephesians 6: 18, praying always with all prayer and supplication in the spirit &c.

Mr. Spencer, chaplain to [the] New York Provincials, and my brother, E. Cleaveland, chaplain to Col. Preble, were present, and there was remarkable attention in the assembly both parts of the day.

After exercise [I] visited Mr. Woodbridge,[17] chaplain to Col. William Williams,[18] sick with an intermittent fever. There seems to be an excellent set of chaplains in the camp.

*3, Monday.* Prayers quite early this morning because the regiment was to be viewed by the General at seven o'clock in the morning. Took my brother E. C. with me and visited John Brainard,[19] chaplain to Col. [John] Johnston of New Jersey regiments, Mr. Ogilvie,[20] chaplain to the regulars, Mr. Spencer, of the New York regiments, and in the afternoon went with the above chaplains, except Ogilvie, to the Connecticut forces where we had an agreeable interview with their four chaplains, viz. Mr. Beckwith, Mr. Eell, Mr. Pomeroy,[21] Mr. Ingersoll, and agreed with them to go in a body together next morning to pay our compliments to His Excellency General Abercrombie. Also agreed to spend some

[17] Possibly the Rev. John Woodbridge (1702–1783) of South Hadley and another Yale graduate.

[18] This Col. Williams commanded a Massachusetts regiment, settled at Pittsfield, and died in 1788. A friend wrote of his marriages: "He married first Miriam Tyler for good sense and got it; secondly, Miss Wells for love and beauty and had it; thirdly, Aunt Hannah Dickinson and got horribly cheated."

[19] Rev. John Brainard (1720–1781) was a Yale graduate of 1746.

[20] Rev. John Ogilvie (1724–1774) was a Yale man but a Church of England chaplain to the Royal American regiment.

[21] Rev. Benjamin Pomeroy (1704–1784) was Yale graduate of 1733.

time in prayer, the Connecticut chaplains by themselves, and the Boston, New Jersey and New York chaplains as many as could (as they were tented near to one another) by themselves.

*4, Tuesday.* This morning after prayers and breakfast, Mr. Beckwith, Mr. Eell, Mr. Pomeroy, Mr. Ingersoll, Mr. Brainard, Mr. Spencer, Mr. Forbush, my brother and myself went to the General's tent and paid our compliments to him. Mr. Beckwith made a short speech or address to him in the name of the whole. He treated us very kindly, told us he hoped we would teach the people their duty and to be courageous, told us a story of a chaplain in Germany where he was that just before the action the chaplain told the soldiers that he had not time to say much, and therefore all he should say would be in these words: be courageous for no cowards would go to Heaven.

The General treated us with a bowl of punch and a bottle of wine, and then we took our leave of him. In the afternoon Morrill of Col. Nichols' regiment, Mr. Brainard, Mr. Forbush, Mr. Woodbridge, my brother and myself met under Col. Ruggles' bower. Mr. Morrill prayed first excellently well after a psalm, Mr. Brainard prayed very affectionately and seriously, and then after another psalm I gave a word of exhortation and dismissed them with a blessing. This day we have orders to be in readiness to strike our tents at daybreak and to be on board the batteaus by five in the morning.

*5, Wednesday.* At daybreak the general [order] was beat, when the tents were immediately struck and everything packed up and carried on board, and by five we were rowing our batteaus. The whole army were upon the water, the regulars in the middle column, Col. Preble, Ruggles, Bagley, Williams &c on the right wing, General Lyman, Col. Whiting, Fitch[22] &c on the left, the artillery in the rear of the main body, and Col. [Oliver] Partridge with the Royal [blank] brought up the rear. The Rangers were in the front. We rowed about twenty miles and had orders to draw up with our batteaus to the western shore, where we pitched our tents and lay till about eleven, and then orders came to go all on board and row immediately to the Narrows. Col. Preble was ordered to lead the van of the right wing and to land with his regiment first upon that wing.

*6, Thursday.* By daylight arrived to the entrance of the Narrows, where we halted till the whole army came up and every regiment took his own place according to the General's orders, and then orders came to row immediately up to the Landing and land, where we expected a very warm reception from the enemy's advanced guard. My heart was much inclined to pour out desires to the God of Heaven that He would appear for us and intimidate the

[22]Col. Eleazer Fitch (1726–1796) commanded the 3rd Connecticut regiment. He stood 6′ 3″ tall and weighed 300 pounds. At the outbreak of the Revolution he became a Loyalist and died in Canada.

enemy, and it is wonderful how God appeared for us, for though the enemy had four battalions in the advanced guard and several cannon, yet by nine o'clock in the morning we were all safely landed. The French only fired a few small arms, which did no harm, and then ran off. But as they burnt the bridges over the river, the army marched through the thick woods to go 'round the bend of the river, and when we had marched about two miles we were attacked in the front by about three thousand French and Indians. At hearing the first fire Col. Bagley's regiment, with which I was, were ordered to form to the right and run up to the enemy. There was a very smart engagement for about an hour. My Lord Howe was killed and about 24 men were missing after we came into the camp where we landed, and several brought in wounded. We captivated of the enemy 159, and it was judged that we killed as many more of them.

7, *Friday.* This day they marched out again to build the bridges so as to march down the wagon road and to take possession of the sawmills, where the enemy have some small strength, and about the sun an hour high the army began their march to take possession of the ground near the fort, and a little after sunset General Johnson[23] arrived with his

[23]Gen. Sir William Johnson was Crown Superintendent of Indian Affairs in the Northern Department, and the Iroquois tribes were his special charge. He had been in the field earlier in the war. During the assault on Ticonderoga his Indians were stationed on a nearby hilltop overlooking the fort but too far away for their muskets to be effective.

regiment. What number of Indians he has brought I can't get intelligence. This night I lodged in a batteau and lay very hard upon the barrels.

8, *Saturday*. This morning General Johnson and his Indians marched after the army before sunrise towards Ticonderoga. This has been a most bloody fight. Our troops attempted to force the French entrenchment before the fort with small arms and met with very great loss on our side. Our men acted with the greatest intrepidity and one or two companies of the Highlanders and regulars were almost entirely cut off. Many were slain and many came in wounded, the number of both are not yet known, though it is conjectured that at least a thousand are among the killed and wounded! Capt. Whipple received a ball in his thigh which lodged there. Lieut. [Nathan] Burn[h]am received a mortal wound in his bowels, and Lieut. Low was slain as we suppose; the last that was seen of him he was sitting down with a mortal wound. The conduct is thought to be marvelous strange to order the entrenchment to be forced with small arms when they had cannon not far off, and numbers sufficient to keep the enemy off till we entrenched and placed our cannon and bomb mortars so as to play upon the enemy. Most of our forces retreated towards the landing where the batteaus lay!

An account of the manner our troops attacked the entrenchment, July 8, 1758, per John Cleaveland, chaplain to Col. Bagley:

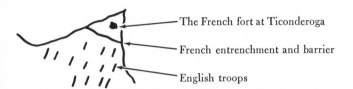

The French fort at Ticonderoga

French entrenchment and barrier

English troops

The work in the angle is Ticonderoga Fort. The cross line the French entrenchment, which did not extend quite from lake to lake. The first strokes under the line are on the right, Rogers; center, light infantry; left, Royal. The next marks from the right (1) Col. Babcock,[24] (2) Col. Doty,[25] (3) Col. Preble, (4) Col. Williams, (5) Col. Bagley, (6) Col. Delancey.[26] The lower marks the regulars, who were to march through those that lay before and make the attack upon the breast work, and to be covered in their retreat, if driven back, by the provincials, but the French not pushing the regulars when they retreated, the provincials were ordered up. The

[24] Col. Henry Babcock (d. 1800) commanded the Rhode Island regiment.

[25] Col. Thomas Doty commanded a Massachusetts regiment.

[26] Col. Oliver Delancey (1718–1785) became a Loyalist and served with the British forces in the Revolution.

Connecticut regiments were not in the fight, except Col. Whiting's and Col. Wooster's who came up about sun an hour high.

*9, Sabbath.* This morning to the general surprise of the whole army, we were ordered to row back in the batteaus, to leave the ground we had possessed, and return to Fort William Henry. We left the ground about 9 o'clock in the morning and arrived to Fort William Henry, full forty miles, before sunset. All disgusted partly on account of our returning and partly on account of our being without much food for three days. This evening Lieut. Burnham was buried, having died upon the water of his wound. I understand he inquired for me, hoping to see me before he died, but I was in another batteau and could not be found, the lake being full of them.

*10, Monday.* This morning orders were given out to make a return of the killed, wounded, and missing, which according to the information I have had amount to eighteen or twenty hundred in the whole army, principally among the regulars and Highlanders. In Col. Bagley's regiment six were killed, two officers and 4 privates; 11 were wounded, Capt. Whipple and 10 privates. This day wherever I went I found people, officers and soldiers, astonished that we left the French ground and lamenting the strange conduct in coming off.

*Lake George, July 11, 1758*

*My dear and loving wife,*

I greatly long to hear of your, my family's and people's welfare. I bless God I have been in good health ever since I left home, and hope by the will of God to see you again, but how soon I know not.

Doubtless you will hear before these lines reach you what a bloody time we have had; however, it may afford some satisfaction to have an account of some particular facts relating to it from one acquainted with the same . . .[He summarizes the attack.] It was a fearful sight to see numbers of men, some with their eyes shot out, their noses cut off by a ball, others shot in their head, neck, shoulders, arms, belly, thighs, legs &c.

Our men kept the ground till sometime in the night, when the cannon was carried back (which indeed was never brought up to the place of engagement) and the troops ordered back to the landing, and next morning to embark and return immediately to the head of the lake to Fort William Henry, where we arrived the same day before sunset much dejected. What were the reasons which influenced our General to order us to return when we had possession of the ground, I don't pretend to relate, but only such things as are known to be matters of fact, without a design of reflection upon any person.

Here we are now, but whether we are to tarry here or go down the lake again or return home I can't tell. Our people never were, and perhaps never were a people, in better spirits for fighting than ours before we left the ground we had gained and returned to this place, but now they seem to have no heart nor courage for anything. A universal dejection appears in everyone's countenance, officers as well as soldiers, and a hundred to one if the bigger part of the army is not sick in a few days, and I am at a loss what encouraging arguments to use with the people to get their spirits up.

Chebacco people here are all alive (except the two lieutenants above mentioned) and as well as other people are.

Remember me to your brother, I want to hear of him, and to Elder [Francis] Choate[27] and the deacons, and desire them in my name to pray much for me, for our army. It is at present the darkest time I ever saw. Remember me to all inquiring friends, and remember me to the throne of grace as I trust I do daily you, my family and people.

*I subscribe yours affectionately,*
John Cleaveland

[27] Francis Choate (1701–1777) was also the uncle of Mrs. Cleaveland.

# 5

## Major Rogers' Journals

*

### *The Raid on St. Francis*
### 1759

# The Raid on St. Francis
## 1759

*Every war produces its heroes, and there can be little doubt that Major Robert Rogers was the authentic hero of the French and Indian War. His exploits not only captured the imagination of the American and English public, but his tactical innovations appealed to the British military. Standing six feet in height — a tall man for those days — he was well muscled and excelled in all feats of strength. In addition he became as adept in woodcraft as the Indians. Consequently he was remarkably able to take care of himself in the wilderness. In his raid on the Indian village of St. Francis only this training and his endurance enabled him to survive.*

*Rogers at twenty-three was living restlessly in New Hampshire when a call for volunteers went out in 1755 to drive the French from Crown Point, on Lake Champlain. He raised a company of more than fifty men and was commissioned a captain. What is remarkable is that he conceived of a scouting task force which could serve the army as eyes and fists in various approaches to the enemy. For this purpose General William Shirley, interim commander-in-chief of Anglo-American forces, commissioned Rogers in 1756 as captain of an independent company of Rangers. Lord Loudoun, the next British commander-in-chief, was convinced of the inadequacy of his regiments of regulars to fight in the wilderness and welcomed the use of unorthodox scouts. He increased the Rangers to several companies of a hundred men each and used them on offensive missions of a hit-and-run character. Rogers wrote a training manual for them, the first of its kind. He was made a major and put in command of all the Rangers, but they were not used as they should have been in the unsuccessful attack on Ticonderoga in 1758.*

*General Amherst, Loudoun's successor, found Rogers indispensable and admired him thoroughly. After the capture in 1759 of Ticonderoga and Crown Point, Amherst acted on Rogers' bold suggestion for a blow against St. Francis, 150 miles beyond Crown Point and between Montreal and Quebec. It was an extremely hazardous venture, but success would achieve several ends: wipe out the prime source of murderous raids that had gone on for generations, frighten off other Indian friends of the French, demonstrate to the French the far-reaching strokes which the English could deliver, and accentuate the fact that the very recent victories of the English were not mere flukes in the war they had been losing since 1755. Rogers and* his Rangers were the only unit that could possibly meet the three requirements of such a dangerous enterprise: getting there without detection, destroying the village, and returning without annihilation.

Rogers was supposed to take 200 men, but for some reason he could not muster more than 182, and on the way more than 40 were sent back. He also had with him officers from the 60th and 80th British regiments who had undoubtedly volunteered. Nevertheless, he was successful in burning the town, but the return journey ahead of hot pursuit was a harrowing experience. During those weeks he lost 35% of his meager force. But let the commander tell his own story, taken from his "Journals," which he either wrote or dictated in London in 1765. First he printed his short report to Amherst on the affair and then went back to enlarge on the exploit, with also some explanatory footnotes. The details are not repetitious, but they are out of order. We have begun the story with Rogers' own narrative, inserted most of the letter to Amherst in quotation marks at the point where the action he describes is pertinent. The result, we trust, is a clearer running account of what happened.

We wish we could record that Major Rogers was properly rewarded and continued a brilliant military career. Neither development took place. He received the surrender of Detroit in 1760 and *returned there three years later with a reinforcement during Chief Pontiac's siege of the fort. Rogers was appointed commandant of Fort Michilimackinac in 1766, but after that all his fortunes were downhill. He died in England in poverty in 1795, a tragic hero. A biography, "Robert Rogers of the Rangers," by John R. Cuneo, was published in 1959.*

*His "Journals" was reprinted abroad in 1769, and in small editions here in 1883 and 1961. An excerpt on the St. Francis raid was included in volume two of the special limited edition of Kenneth Roberts' novel, "Northwest Passage," in 1937.*

*This portrait of Major Rogers published in London
by Thomas Hart in 1776 is imaginary,
but it was very popular and was copied for reproduction
in France and Germany.
No portrait taken from life is known.*

Route of Major Rogers to St. Francis
and His Retreat 1759

0   10   20
miles

Quebec

St. Lawrence River

CANADA

N

Lake St. Peter

St. Francis
destroyed Oct. 6

Sorel

Richelieu River

Yamaska River

St. Francis River

Montreal

Lake Megantic

Lake
Memphremagog

Rogers' forces divided near here

Missisquoi Bay
Arrived Sept. 23

Missisquoi River

Dunbar and
Turner ambushed

Lake Champlain

Winooski River

Androscoggin River

Forty men sent back
Sept. 15

Ammonoosuc River

Saco River

Crown
Point

Left Crown
Point Sept. 13

Coös Intervales

Arrived Oct. 23
Left on Oct. 27

Sebago Lake

Fort
Ticonderoga

Lake George

White River

Connecticut River

White River
Falls

Lake
Winnepesaukee

Falmouth
(Portland)

Wattaquitchy Falls

Merrimack River

Fort No. 4
(Charlestown)
Arrived Oct. 31

Suncook

Portsmouth

Hudson R.

Atlantic

# Major Rogers' Journals

THUS were we employed till the 12th of September [1759], when the General, exasperated at the treatment which Capt. Kennedy had met with, who had been sent with a party as a flag of truce to the St. Francis Indians, with proposals of peace to them, and was by them made a prisoner with the whole party; this ungenerous inhumane treatment determined the General to chastize these savages with some severity and, in order to do it, I received from him the following orders, viz.

"You are this night to set out with the detachment as ordered yesterday, viz. of 200 men, which you will take under your command and proceed to Missisquoi Bay,[1] from whence you will march and attack the enemy's settlement on the south side of the River St. Lawrence in such a manner as you shall judge most effectual to disgrace the enemy, and for the success and honor of His Majesty's arms.

"Remember the barbarities that have been committed by the enemy's Indian scoundrels on every occasion where they had an opportunity of showing their infamous cruelties on the King's subjects, which they have done without mercy. Take your revenge, but don't forget that though those villains have dastardly and promiscuously murdered the

[1] Missisquoi Bay is at the northeastern end of Lake Champlain and stretches into the Province of Quebec.

women and children of all ages, it is my orders that no women or children are killed or hurt.

"When you have executed your intended service, you will return with your detachment to camp or join me wherever the army may be.

Your's &c.

Jeff. Amherst"

Camp at Crown Point
Sept. 13, 1759.

To Major Rogers.

(That this expedition might be carried on with the utmost secrecy after the plan of it was concerted the day before my march, it was put into public orders that I was to march a different way, at the same time I had private instructions to proceed directly to St. Francis.)

In pursuance of the above orders, I set out the same evening with a detachment [of 182]; and as to the particulars of my proceedings, and the great difficulties we met with in effecting our design, the reader is referred to the letter I wrote to General Amherst upon my return. . .

I cannot forbear here making some remarks on the difficulties and distresses which attended us in effecting this enterprise upon St. Francis, which is situated within three miles of the River St. Lawrence, in the middle of Canada, about halfway between Montreal and Quebec. Capt. Williams[2] of the Royal

[2] Actually Capt. Samuel Willyamos of the 60th or Royal American regiment.

regiment was, the fifth day of our march, accidentally burnt with gun powder and several men hurt, which together with some sick returned back to Crown Point, to the number of forty, under the care of Capt. Williams, who returned with great reluctance.

It was extremely difficult while we kept the water (and which retarded our progress very much) to pass undiscovered by the enemy, who were then cruising in great numbers upon the Lake; and had prepared certain vessels on purpose to decoy any party of ours that might come that way, armed with all manner of machines and implements for their destruction; but we happily escaped their snares of this kind and landed (as has been mentioned) the tenth day at Missisquoi Bay.

Here, that I might with more certainty know whether my boats (with which I had left provision sufficient to carry us back to Crown Point) were discovered by the enemy, I left two trusty Indians to lie at a distance in sight of the boats and there to stay till I came back, except the enemy found them; in which latter case they were with all possible speed to follow on my track and give me intelligence. It happened the second day after I left them that these two Indians came up to me in the evening and informed me that about 400 French had discovered and taken my boats, and that about one half of them were hotly pursuing my track. This unlucky circumstance (it may well be supposed) put us into some consternation. Should the enemy overtake us, and we get the better of them in an encounter, yet being so far advanced into their country where no reinforcement could possibly relieve us, and where they could be supported by any numbers they pleased, afforded us little hopes of escaping their hands. Our boats being taken cut off all hope of a retreat by them; besides, the loss of our provisions left with them, of which we knew we should have great need at any rate in case we survived, was a melancholy consideration.

It was, however, resolved to prosecute our design at all adventures and, when we had accomplished it, to attempt a retreat (the only possible way we could think of) by way of No. 4;[3] and that we might not be destroyed by famine in our return, I dispatched Lieut. [Andrew] McMullen by land to Crown Point to desire of the General to relieve me with provision at Ammonoosuc River at the end of Coös Intervales on Connecticut River,[4] that being the way I should return, if at all, and the pace being about sixty miles from No. 4, then the most northerly English settlement. This being done, we determined if possible to outmarch our pursuers and effect our design upon St. Francis before they could overtake us.

We marched nine days through wet sunken ground; the water most of the way near a foot deep,

[3] No. 4 was a small fort at modern Charlestown, N. H., on the Connecticut River.

[4] The Ammonoosuc River empties into the Connecticut River on the east side, opposite the mouth of Wells River, at the Lower Cohase Intervales. The towns of Woodsville, N. H., and Wells River, Vt., are on the site today.

it being a spruce bog. When we encamped at night, we had no way to secure ourselves from the water but by cutting the boughs of trees and with them erecting a kind of hammocks. We commonly began our march a little before day and continued it till after dark at night.

The tenth day after leaving Missisquoi Bay, we came to a river about fifteen miles above the town of St. Francis to the south of it; and the town being on the opposite or east side of it, we were obliged to ford it, which was attended by no small difficulty, the water being five feet deep and the current swift. I put the tallest men upstream, and then holding to each other, we got over with the loss of several of our guns, some of which we recovered by diving to the bottom for them. . .

"The twenty-second day after my departure from Crown Point [October 5], I came in sight of the Indian town St. Francis in the evening, which I discovered from a tree that I climbed at about three miles distance. Here I halted my party which now consisted of 142 men, officers included. . . At eight o'clock this evening I left the detachment and took with me Lieut. Turner and Ensign Avery and went to reconnoitre the town, which I did to my satisfaction, and found the Indians in a high frolic or dance. I returned to my party at two o'clock and at three marched it to within five hundred yards of the town, where I lightened the men of their packs and formed them for the attack.

"At half hour before sunrise I surprised the town when they were all fast asleep on the right, left, and center, which was done with so much alacrity by both the officers and men that the enemy had not time to recover themselves, or take arms for their defense, till they were chiefly destroyed, except some few of them who took to the water. About forty of my people pursued them, who destroyed such as attempted to make their escape that way, and sunk both them and their boats. A little after sunrise I set fire to all their houses except three in which there was corn that I reserved for the use of the party.

"The fire consumed many of the Indians who had concealed themselves in the cellars and lofts of their houses. About seven o'clock in the morning the affair was completely over, in which time we had killed at least two hundred Indians and taken twenty of their women and children prisoners, fifteen of whom I let go their own way and five I brought with me, viz two Indian boys and three Indian girls. I likewise retook five English captives which I also took under my care."

This nation of Indians was notoriously attached to the French and had for near a century past harrassed the frontiers of New England, killing people of all ages and sexes in a most barbarous manner, at a time when they did not in the least suspect them; and to my own knowledge in six years time carried into captivity and killed on the before mentioned frontiers 400 persons. We found in the town hanging on poles over their doors, &c. about 600 scalps, mostly English.

"When I had paraded my detachment, I found I had Capt. [Amos] Ogden badly wounded in his body, but not so as to hinder him from doing his duty. I had also six men slightly wounded and one Stockbridge Indian killed.

"I ordered my people to take corn out of the reserved houses for their subsistence home, there being no other provision there, and whilst they were loading themselves I examined the prisoners and captives who gave me the following intelligence: That a party of 300 French and some Indians were about four miles down the river below us; and that our boats were waylaid, that a party of 200 French and fifteen Indians had, three days before I attacked the town, gone up the river Wigwam Martinique,[5] supposing that was the place I intended to attack; whereupon I called the officers together to consult the safety of our return, who were of opinion there was no other way for us to return with safety but by No. 4 on Connecticut River. I marched the detachment eight days in a body that way; and when provisions grew scarce, near Memphremagog Lake, I divided the detachment into small companies, putting proper guides to each, who were to assemble at the mouth of Ammonoosuc River, as I expected provisions would be brought there for our relief, not knowing which way I should return."

[5] Now called the Yamaska River.

It is hardly possible to describe the grief and consternation of those of us who came to Coös Intervales. Upon our arrival there (after so many days tedious march over steep rocky mountains or through wet dirty swamps, with the terrible attendants of fatigue and hunger) to find that here was no relief for us, where we had encouraged ourselves that we should find it, and have our distresses alleviated; for notwithstanding the officer I had dispatched to the General discharged his trust with great expedition, and in nine days arrived at Crown Point, which was a hundred miles through the woods, and the General without delay sent Lieut. [Samuel] Stephens to No. 4 with orders to take provisions up the river to the place I had appointed and there wait as long as there was any hopes of my returning; yet the officer that was sent being an indolent fellow, tarried at the place but two days, when he returned, taking all the provisions back with him, about two hours before our arrival. Finding a fresh fire burning in his camp, I fired guns to bring him back, which guns he heard but would not return, supposing we were an enemy.

(This gentleman, for this piece of conduct, was broke by a general courtmartial and rendered incapable of sustaining any office in His Majesty's service for the future: a poor reward, however, for the distress and anguish thereby occasioned to so many brave men, to some of which it proved fatal, they actually dying with hunger.)

"Two days after we parted, Ensign Avery of Fitch's[6] fell in on my track and followed in my rear; and a party of the enemy came upon them and took seven of his party prisoners, two of whom that night made their escape and came in to me next morning. Avery, with the remainder of his party, joined mine and came with me to the Coös Intervales where I left them with Lieut. Grant. . ."

Our distress upon this occasion was truly inexpressible; our spirits, greatly depressed by the hunger and fatigues we had already suffered, now almost entirely sunk within us, seeing no resource left, nor any reasonable ground to hope that we should escape a most miserable death by famine. At length I came to a resolution to push as fast as possible towards No. 4, leaving the remains of my party, now unable to march further, to get such wretched subsistance as the barren wilderness could afford, till I could get relief to them, which I engaged to do within ten days. I, with Capt. Ogden, one Ranger, and a captive Indian boy, embarked upon a raft we had made of dry pine trees.

The current carried us down the stream in the middle of the river, where we endeavored to keep our wretched vessel by such paddles as we had made out of small trees, or spires split and hewed. The second day we reached White River Falls and very narrowly escaped being carried over them by the

[6] Probably Col. Eleazer Fitch's 3rd Connecticut regiment mentioned in John Cleaveland's narrative.

current. Our little remains of strength, however, enabled us to land and to march by them. At the bottom of these falls, while Capt. Ogden and the Ranger hunted for red squirrels for refreshment, who had the good fortune likewise to kill a partridge, I attempted forming a new raft for our further conveyance. Being not able to cut down trees, I burnt them down and then burnt them off at proper lengths. This was our third day's work after leaving our companions.

The next day we got our materials together and completed our raft, and floated with the stream again till we came to Ottauquechee Falls, which are about fifty yards in length. Here we landed, and by a wreath made of hazel bushes Capt. Ogden held the raft till I went to the bottom, prepared to swim in and board it when it came down, and if possible paddle it ashore, this being our only resource for life, as we were not able to make a third raft in case we had lost this. I had the good fortune to succeed, and the next morning we embarked and floated down the stream to within a small distance of No. 4 where we found some men cutting timber, who gave us the first relief and assisted us to the fort, from whence I dispatched a canoe with provisions which reached the men at Coös four days after, which (agreeable to my engagement) was the tenth after I left them.

Two days after my arrival at No. 4 I went with other canoes, loaded with provisions, up the river myself for the relief of others of my party that might be coming in that way, having hired some of the inhabitants to assist me in this affair. (I met several different parties: as Lieut. [Abernathan] Curgill, Lieut. [George] Campbell, Lieut. [Jacob] Farrington, and Sergeant Evans, with their respective division, and sent canoes farther up for the relief of such as might be still behind and coming this way. Some I met who escaped from Dunbar's and Turner's party, who were overtaken, being upwards of twenty in number, and were mostly killed or taken by the enemy.) I likewise sent expresses to Suncook and Penacoock upon Merrimack River, that any who should chance to straggle that way might be assisted; and provisions were sent up said rivers accordingly.

On my return to No. 4 I waited a few days to refresh such of my party I had been able to collect together. . . As soon as my party were refreshed, such as were able I marched to Crown Point, where I arrived Dec. 1, 1759; and upon examination found that since our leaving the ruins of St. Francis I had lost three officers, viz. Lieut. [James] Dunbar of Gage's Light Infantry, Lieut. [George] Turner of the Rangers, and Lieut. Jenkins of the Provincials, and forty-six sergeants and privates.

# 6

## Anne Grant's Memoirs

*

### *The Children of Albany*
### 1762-68

# The Children of Albany
## 1762-68

When Duncan MacVicar was ordered to America with his Scotch regiment, his wife and three-year-old daughter Anne followed in 1758 and settled at Claverack, New York, on the Hudson River. There Anne was taught to read by her mother and learned the Dutch language of her neighbors. She was a precocious child and not only read early and widely, but observed and remembered people with ease. Her father, she said later, fought at Ticonderoga. MacVicar transferred to the 55th regiment as an ensign, or second lieutenant, and was appointed quartermaster.

When he was ordered to the fort at Oswego on Lake Ontario in 1761, he obtained permission to take his wife and daughter on the supply boats up the Mohawk River, down Wood Creek to Lake Oneida, and down the Oswego River. The family remained at Fort Oswego during the winter, but returned in 1762 to Albany, a town of less than 2000 population.

Now Anne met a neighbor, Madam Schuyler, the portly widow of Col. Philip Schuyler. As Margaretta Schuyler she had married her cousin in

*1720 and was related to most of the prominent
families in the area. She lived at the Flats, a farm
having a two-mile frontage on the Hudson just
north of town. She owned another house in Albany
located at the corner of State and Pearl Streets.
Madam Schuyler was 61 years old and always had
relatives living with her. Anne MacVicar became
a devoted young companion, entranced by her
"aunt's" conversation, her generous gestures, and
her household. From her she learned readily about
Albany life, especially the life of children. She
witnessed the excitement of the military over Chief
Pontiac's uprising in the West in 1763, and the
Stamp Act controversy in 1765. For six years she
lived near the Flats or with Mrs. Schuyler in town.*

*Her father resigned his commission in 1765 and
went on half pay, turning his attention to the
development of a tract of land in modern Vermont
for settlement. His efforts, however, were clouded
by the quarrel between New York and New Hampshire over title to the region that ultimately became
Vermont, and in gloom Mr. MacVicar decided to
return to Scotland. In 1768 Anne had to leave her
affectionate friends, young and old, rich and poor,
black and white, but she never forgot her youthful
life in America, and through the mist of receding
years it grew increasingly idyllic.*

*In 1779 she married James Grant, a minister, and had a dozen children, of whom four died young. After her husband died in 1801, her interest in writing developed into a means of a livelihood. Mrs. Grant published some poems and three volumes of letters. She knew Sir Walter Scott and other literary figures of the day. In 1808 appeared her highly successful "Memoirs of an American Lady," a tribute to Madam Schuyler and a description of life in New York before the Revolution. Her relation of historical events contains some errors, but no one has disputed her observations of customs and manners of the Albany young people at the time of her residence among them. Despite her overblown prose at times, they form the only such description we have. Since she detailed the amusements of youth in two different parts of her memoirs, we have had to re-arrange some paragraphs to unify her account.*

*Mrs. Grant died in Edinburgh in 1838 at the age of eighty-three, having outlived all her children except one son. Her book has been reprinted eight times, but last in 1903.*

ANNE GRANT

*Mrs. Grant in 1825, from a miniature by K. Macleay*
*engraved by H. Robinson*

# Anne Grant's Memoirs

THE foundations of both friendship and still ten-
derer attachments were here laid very early by
an institution which I always thought had been peculiar to Albany, till I found in Dr. Moore's *View of
Society*[1] on the Continent an account of a similar
custom subsisting in Geneva. The children of the
town were all divided into companies, as they called
them, from five to six years of age till they became
marriageable. How those companies first originated,
or what were their exact regulations, I cannot say;
though I, belonging to none, occasionally mixed
with several, yet always as a stranger, though I
spoke their current language fluently.

Every company contained as many boys as girls.
But I do not know that there was any limited number; only this I recollect, that a boy and a girl of
each company who were older, cleverer, or had some
other preëminence above the rest, were called heads
of the company and as such, obeyed by the others.
Whether they were voted in, or attained their preëminence by a tacit acknowledgment of their superiority, I know not, but however it was attained it
was never disputed. The company of little children
had also their heads. All the children of the same

[1] Dr. John Moore (1729–1802) published in 1779 *A View
of Society and Manners in France, Switzerland, and Germany*,
in two volumes.

age were not in one company; there were at least
three or four of equal ages, who had a strong rivalry
with each other; and children of different ages in
the same family belonged to different companies.
Wherever there is human nature there will be a
degree of emulation, strife, and a desire to lessen
others, that we may exalt ourselves. Dispassionate
as my friends comparatively were, and bred up in
the highest attainable candor and innocence, they
regarded the company most in competition with
their own with a degree of jealous animosity.

Each company at a certain time of the year went
in a body, to gather a particular kind of berries, to
the hills. It was a sort of annual festival, attended
with religious punctuality. Every company had a
uniform for this purpose; that is to say, very pretty
light baskets made by the Indians with lids and
handles, which hung over the arm, and were adorned
with various colors. One company would never
allow the least degree of taste to the other in this instance, and was sure to vent its whole stock of spleen
in decrying the rival baskets. Nor would they ever
admit that the rival company gathered near so much
fruit on these excursions as they did. The parents
of these children seemed very much to encourage
this manner of marshalling and dividing themselves.

Every child was permitted to entertain the whole
company on its birthday and once besides during
winter and spring. The master and mistress of the

family always were bound to go from home on these occasions, while some old domestic was left to attend and watch over them, with an ample provision of tea, chocolate, preserved and dried fruits, nuts, and cakes of various kinds, to which was added cider or a syllabub,[2] for these young friends met at four and did not part till nine or ten and amused themselves with the utmost gaiety and freedom in any way their fancy dictated. I speak from hearsay, for no person that does not belong to the company is ever admitted to these meetings: other children or young people visit occasionally and are civilly treated, but they admit of no intimacies beyond their company.

The consequence of these exclusive and early intimacies was that grown up, it was reckoned a sort of apostasy to marry out of one's company. And indeed it did not often happen. The girls, from the example of their mothers rather than any compulsion, became very early notable and industrious, being constantly employed in knitting stockings and making clothes for the family and slaves; they even made all the boys' clothes. This was the more necessary as all articles of clothing were extremely dear. Though all the necessaries of life and some luxuries abounded, money as yet was a scarce commodity. This industry was the more to be admired as children were here indulged to a degree that in our

---

[2] Or sillabub, which is wine or cider mixed with milk to form a soft curd.

vitiated state of society would have rendered them good for nothing. But there, where ambition, vanity, and the more turbulent passions were scarce awakened; where pride, founded on birth or any external preëminence, was hardly known; and where the affections flourished fair and vigorous, unchecked by the thorns and thistles with which our minds are cursed in a more advanced state of refinement, affection restrained parents from keeping their children at a distance and inflicting harsh punishment . . . They were tenderly cherished and early taught that they owed all their enjoyments to the divine source of beneficence, to whom they were finally accountable for their actions; for the rest they were very much left to nature and permitted to range about at full liberty in their earliest years, covered in summer with some slight and cheap garb which merely kept the sun from them, and in the winter with some warm habit in which convenience only was consulted. Their dress of ceremony was never put on but when their *company* was assembled. . . .

The children returned the fondness of their parents with such tender affection that they feared giving them pain as much as ours do punishment, and very rarely wounded their feelings by neglect or rude answers. Yet the boys were often willful and giddy at a certain age, the girls being sooner tamed and domesticated.

These youths were apt, whenever they could carry a gun (which they did at a very early period), to follow some favorite Negro to the woods and, while he was employed in felling trees, range the whole day in search of game, to the neglect of all intellectual improvement, and contract a love of savage liberty which might, and in some instances did, degenerate into licentious and idle habits. Indeed, there were three stated periods in the year when for a few days young and old, masters and slaves, were abandoned to unruly enjoyment and neglected every serious occupation for pursuits of this nature . . .

On the banks of these lakes were large tracts of ground covered with a plant taller and more luxuriant than the wild carrot,[3] but something resembling it, on the seeds of which the pigeons feed all the summer while they are breeding and rearing their young. When they pass in spring, which they always do in the same track, they go in great numbers and are very fat. Their progression northward and southward begins always about the vernal and autumnal equinoxes; and it is this that renders the carnage so great when they pass over inhabited districts . . . pigeons in pies and soups and every way they could be dressed were the food of the inhabitants. These were immediately succeeded by wild geese and ducks, which concluded the carnival for that season, to be renewed in September.

About six weeks after the passage of these birds, sturgeon of a large size and in great quantity made their appearance in the river. Now the same ardor

[3] Probably the cow parsnip.

seemed to pervade all ages in pursuit of this new object. Every family had a canoe, and on this occasion all were launched; and these persevering fishers traced the course of the sturgeon up the river, followed them by torchlight, and often continued two nights upon the water, never returning till they had loaded their canoes with this valuable fish, and many other very excellent in their kinds that come up the river at the same time. The sturgeon not only furnished them with good part of their food in the summer months, but was pickled or dried for future use or exportation . . .

In spring eight or ten of the young people of one company or related to each other, young men and maidens, would set out together in a canoe on a kind of rural excursion, of which amusement was the object. Yet so fixed were their habits of industry that they never failed to carry their work-baskets with them, not as a form but as an ingredient necessarily mixed with their pleasure. They had no attendants and steered a devious course of four, five, or perhaps more miles till they arrived at some of the beautiful islands with which this river abounded, or at some sequestered spot on its banks where delicious wild fruits or particular conveniences for fishing afford some attraction.

There they generally arrived at nine or ten o'clock, having set out in the cool and early hour of sunrise. Often they met another party going, perhaps, to a different place and joined them or induced them to take their route. A basket with tea, sugar, and the other usual provisions for breakfast, with the apparatus for cooking it; a little rum and fruit for making cool weak punch, the usual beverage in the middle of the day; and now and then some cold pastry was the sole provision; for the great affair was to depend on the sole exertions of the boys in procuring fish, wild ducks, etc. for their dinner. They were all, like Indians, ready and dexterous with the axe, gun, etc.

Whenever they arrived at their destination, they sought out a dry and beautiful spot opposite to the river, and in an instant with their axes cleared so much superfluous shade or shrubbery as left a semi-circular opening, above which they bent and twined the boughs so as to form a pleasant bower, while the girls gathered dried branches, to which one of the youths soon set fire with gun powder, and the breakfast, a very regular and cheerful one, occupied an hour or two; the young men then set out to fish or perhaps shoot birds, and the maidens sat busily down to their work, singing and conversing with all the ease and gaiety the bright serenity of the atmosphere and beauty of the surrounding scene were calculated to inspire . . .

After the sultry hours had been thus employed, the boys brought their tribute from the river or the wood, and found a rural meal prepared by their fair companions, among whom were generally their sisters and the chosen of their hearts. After dinner they all set out together to gather wild strawberries, or whatever other fruit was in season, for it was accounted a reflection to come home empty-handed. When wearied of this amusement, they either drank tea in their bower or, returning, landed at some friend's on the way to partake of that refreshment. . .

Another of their summer amusements was going to the bush, which was thus managed: a party of young people set out in little open carriages, something in the form of a gig, of which every family had one; every one carried something with him, as in these cases there was no hunting to add provision. One brought wine for negus,[4] another tea and coffee of a superior quality, a third a pigeon pie; in short, every one brought something, no matter how trifling, for there was no emulation about the extent of the contribution.

In this same bush there were spots to which the poorer members of the community retired, to work their way with patient industry, through much privation and hardship compared to the plenty and comfort enjoyed by the rest. They perhaps could only afford to have one Negro woman, whose children as they grew up became to their master a source of plenty and ease; but in the meantime the good man wrought hard himself, with a little occasional aid sent him by his friends. He had plenty of the necessaries of life, but no luxuries. His wife and

[4] A mixture of wine, hot water, sugar, nutmeg, and lemon juice.

daughter milked the cows and wrought at the hay, and his house was on a smaller scale than the older settlers had theirs, yet he had always one neatly furnished room, a very clean house with a pleasant portico before it, generally a fine stream beside his dwelling, and some Indian wigwams near it. . . .

The young parties, or sometimes elder ones, who set out on this woodland excursion, had no fixed destination; they went generally in the forenoon and when they were tired of going on the ordinary road turned into the bush, and whenever they saw an inhabited spot, with the appearance of which they were pleased, went in with all the ease of intimacy and told them they were come to spend the afternoon there. The good people, not in the least surprised at this incursion, very calmly opened the reserved apartment or, if it were very hot, received them in the portico.

The guests produced their stores, and they boiled their teakettle and provided cream, nuts, or any peculiar dainty of the woods which they chanced to have, and they always furnished bread and butter, which they had excellent of their kinds. They were invited to share the collation, which they did with great ease and frankness; then dancing or any other amusement that struck their fancy succeeded. They sauntered about the bounds in the evening, and returned (home) by moonlight . . .

In winter the river, frozen to a great depth, formed the principal road through the country and was the scene of all those amusements of skating and sledge[5] races common to the north of Europe. They used in great parties to visit their friends at a distance and, having an excellent and hardy breed of horses, flew from place to place over the snow or ice in these sledges with incredible rapidity, stopping a little while at every house they came to and always well received, whether acquainted with the owners or not. The night never impeded these travelers, for the atmosphere was so pure and serene that the snow so reflected the moon and starlight that the nights exceeded the days in beauty.

In town all the boys were extravagantly fond of a diversion that to us would appear a very odd and childish one. The great street of the town, in the midst of which stood all the churches and public buildings, sloped down from the hill on which the fort stood towards the river; between the buildings was an unpaved carriage road, the foot-path beside the houses being the only part of the street which was paved. In winter this sloping descent continued for more than a quarter of a mile, acquired firmness from the frost, and became extremely slippery. Then the amusement commenced.

Every boy and youth in town, from eight to eighteen, had a little low sledge made with a rope like a bridle to the front, by which it could be

[5] By sledge here she means what we call a sleigh or cutter, drawn by a horse. In the next paragraphs by sledge she means a child's sled.

dragged after one by the hand. On this one or two at most could sit, and this sloping descent being made smooth as a looking glass by sliders' sledges, etc., perhaps a hundred at once set out in succession from the top of this street, each seated in his little sledge with the rope in hand which, drawn to the right or left, served to guide him. He pushed it off with a little stick, as one would launch a boat, and then with the most astonishing velocity, precipitated by the weight of the owner, the little machine glided past and was at the lower end of the street in an instant . . . to a young Albanian sleighing, as he called it, was one of the first joys of life, though attended by the drawback of walking to the top of the declivity dragging his sledge every time he renewed his flight . . .

Now there remains another amusement to be described which I mention with reluctance . . . The young men now and then spent a convivial evening at a tavern together where, from the extreme cheapness of liquor, their bills (even when they committed an occasional excess) were moderate. Either to lessen the expense of the supper, or from the pure love of what they styled a frolic, they never failed to steal either a roasting pig or a fat turkey for this festive occasion. The town was the scene of these depredations, which never extended beyond it . . .

The dexterity of the theft consisting in climbing over very high walls, watching to steal in when the Negroes went down to feed the horse or cow, or making a clandestine entrance at some window or aperture, breaking up doors was quite out of rule and rarely ever resorted to. These exploits were always performed in the darkest nights; if the owner heard a noise in his stables, he usually ran down with a cudgel and laid it without mercy on any culprit he could overtake. This was either dexterously avoided or patiently borne . . . Nothing was more common than to find one's brothers or nephews amongst these pillagers. . . .

To return to the boys, as all young men were called here till they married. Thus early trained to a love of sylvan sports, their characters were unfolded by contingencies. In this infant society penal laws lay dormant, and every species of coercion was unknown. In consequence of this singular mode of associating together little exclusive parties of children of both sexes, which has been already mentioned, endearing intimacies formed in the age of playful innocence were the precursors of more tender attachments . . .

If the temper of the youth was rash and impetuous, and his fair one gentle and complying, they frequently formed a rash and precipitate union without consulting their relations, when perhaps the elder of the two was not above seventeen. This was very quietly borne by the parties aggrieved. The relations of both parties met and with great calmness consulted on what was to be done. The father of the youth or the damsel, which ever it was who had most wealth, or fewest children, brought home the young couple; and the new married man immediately set about a trading venture, which was renewed every season, till he had the means of providing a home of his own. Meantime the increase of the younger family did not seem an inconvenience, but rather a source of delight to the old people; and an arrangement begun from necessity was often continued through choice for many years after. . . .

Thus it was in the case of unauthorized marriages. In the more ordinary course of things, love, which makes labor light, tamed these young hunters and transformed them into diligent and laborious traders, for the nature of their trade included very severe labor. When one of the boys was deeply smitten, his fowling piece and fishing rod were at once relinquished. He demanded of his father forty or at most fifty dollars, a Negro boy, and a canoe; all of a sudden he assumed the brow of care and solicitude and began to smoke, a precaution absolutely necessary to repel aguish damps and troublesome insects. He arrayed himself in a habit very little differing from that of the aborigines into whose bounds he was about to penetrate, and in short commenced Indian trader: that strange amphibious animal who uniting the acute senses, strong instincts, and unconquerable patience and fortitude of the savage with the art, policy, and inventions of the European, encountered in the pursuit of gain dangers and difficulties equal to those described in the romantic legends of chivalry. . . .

The joy that the return of these youths occasioned

was proportioned to the anxiety their perilous journey had produced. In some instances the union of the lovers immediately took place before the next career of gainful hardships commenced. But the more cautious went to New York in winter, disposed of their peltry, purchased a larger cargo and another slave and canoe. The next year they laid out the profits of their former adventures in flour and provisions, the staple of the province; this they disposed of at the Bermuda Islands, where they generally purchased one of those light sailing, cedar schooners, for building of which those islanders are famous, and proceeding to the Leeward Islands loaded it with a cargo of rum, sugar and molasses. They were now ripened into men and considered as active and useful members of society, possessing a stake in the common weal.

The young adventurer had generally finished this process by the time he was one, or at most, two and twenty. He now married, or if married before, which pretty often was the case, brought home his wife to a house of his own. Either he kept his schooner and, loading her with produce, sailed up and down the river all summer, and all winter disposed of the cargoes he obtained to more distant settlers; or he sold her, purchased European goods, and kept a store. Otherwise he settled in the country and became as diligent in his agricultural pursuits as if he had never known any other.

# 7

## Lieut. Jehu Hay's Diary

*

*Under Siege in Detroit*
1763

# Under Siege in Detroit
## 1763

A native of Chester, Pennsylvania, Jehu Hay obtained a commission in 1758 in the 60th or Royal American regiment, a huge British unit of four battalions of one thousand men each. It had been created especially to attract American volunteers and other "foreigners." Many of its officers were Swiss mercenaries.

Hay was promoted to lieutenant and went out to Detroit in the summer of 1762 under Major Henry Gladwin with a second company of Royal Americans to augment the one company in garrison. Thus he was on duty when Pontiac, an Ottawa war chief, united the tribes in the three villages on the Detroit River—Hurons, Potawatomies, and Ottawas— against the British. Without a doubt Pontiac was encouraged by some of the local French inhabitants, whose lies about the coming of French troops fueled the dissatisfactions of the Indians over dealing with English traders and troops at Fort Detroit since their arrival in 1760.

Incidents moved to a climax as the Indians returned from their wintering grounds to their villages in the spring of 1763. Pontiac developed a deceptive plot for seizing the fort by surprise, but Major Gladwin learned of it and spoiled his plan. The warriors kept the fort under siege for six months but could not frighten the commandant or starve out the garrison and traders. Two sailing ships, which could not be fought from canoes, brought supplies from Niagara. The Indians would not make use of their overpowering numbers to chop through the Detroit stockade because that kind of assault required the certain sacrifice of many warriors in the process, and the red men lacked that kind of discipline. The English were relatively safe within their walls, but hardly comfortable or cheerful. Each week brought news of the capture of another fort. Of the ten forts west of the Niagara-Pittsburgh line, all of them were taken by the Indians except Detroit. What is astonishing is the staying power of the Indians in conducting the siege, a form of warfare they rarely practiced.

Gladwin's one attempt at a major offensive was almost disastrous. After the arrival of Captain Dalyell with a reinforcement, he persuaded Gladwin to let him make an attack on Pontiac's Ottawa village three miles up river. The chief learned of the column's approach and spread his warriors in a U formation to envelop the troops as they reached the bridge over Parent's Creek. Only the quick action of Major Robert Rogers saved the detachment of

*248 from annihilation, although Hay does not give him credit. Casualties amounted to better than 25% of the force.*

*After that the English continued their waiting game. Pontiac's allies began to pull away in disgust over his lack of success. The time for winter hunting and trapping drew near. After snow fell at the end of October even Pontiac realized he could not keep up the siege and drifted off southward. His final disappointment was word that he could expect no help from French troops from Illinois. Suddenly the gates of the fort swung open. The local French protested their innocence and declared they had been held in terror by the savages. Gladwin sent away the troops he could not feed during the winter, and life settled back into grim reality. Back at eastern headquarters, General Thomas Gage readied two punitive expeditions for 1764.*

*Lieut. Hay did his duty regularly and performed creditably on two minor sorties. He also kept a diary that is one of two daily records of the Indian uprising. The other journal, kept by Robert Navarre, a French resident outside the fort, was published as a Lakeside Classic in 1958 under the title of "The Siege of Detroit in 1763." It ends abruptly on July 31. Hay's diary shows how the dangerous and tense days were passed; it gives one a sense of being there, imprisoned by the stockade. He spells the chief's*

*name with a "d" rather than a "t" because that is
the way it sounded to him.*

*Despite his experience in the fort, Hay liked
Detroit and stayed on. One reason was that he had
fallen in love with a local French girl, Julie Marie
Réaume, whom he married in 1764 when she was
sixteen. They had several children, although only
two sons and a daughter are known to have reached
maturity. Hay was appointed commissary for
Indian affairs in 1766, and it was he who escorted
Pontiac to Oswego, N.Y., that summer for final
treaty making with Sir William Johnson.*

*In 1776 Hay was named deputy Indian agent
and a major of Detroit militia. Two years later he
marched with Col. Henry Hamilton to Vincennes (Indiana), where they were captured by George Rogers
Clark's American force early in 1779. Both men
were sent to Williamsburg, Va., and lodged in jail.
When they were released on parole in October 1780,
they spent the winter in British-held New York City.
Exchanged in 1781 the two officers proceeded to
England. Hamilton was made lieutenant governor of
Quebec in 1782, and Hay succeeded him as lieutenant
governor of Detroit. However, he was held in Lower
Canada for several months and then fell ill in Mon-
treal. As a result he did not return home and rejoin
his family until July 1784. A year later he died in
Detroit and was buried there. His widow died in 1795.*

*Detroit was the scene of another Lakeside Classic, published in 1940. Entitled "War on the Detroit," it contained two documents: the journal of Thomas Verchères de Boucherville from 1803 to 1819, covering the recapture of Detroit by the British in 1812; and* The Capitulation, *an account of Detroit's surrender as seen by an Ohio volunteer.*

*Hay's diary was not known to Francis Parkman before he completed his "History of the Conspiracy of Pontiac," published in 1851. It was purchased from a bookseller in London probably in the 1850's by an American collector, William Menzies. In 1860 the diary, with author unknown, was printed by J. Munsell at Albany in a surprisingly limited edition of only a hundred copies for subscribers, so that it was little known. At the sale of the Menzies library in 1876, the manuscript was acquired by Joseph Drexel of Philadelphia. Not until 1928 was the diary keeper identified as Lieut. Hay. The Clements Library bought the diary in 1936. It was invaluable to this editor as author of "Pontiac and the Indian Uprising," 1947, for the flavor of the time.*

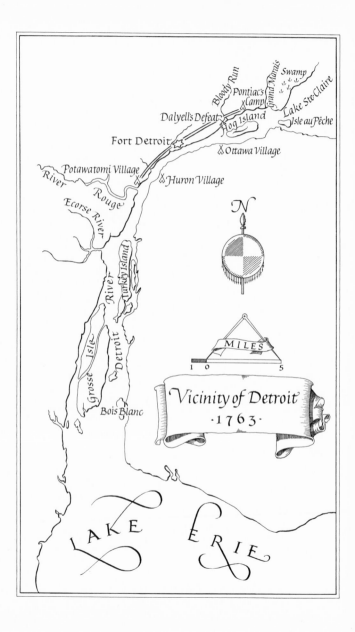

Bloody Run

Pontiac's Camp

Grand Marais Swamp

Dalyell's Defeat

Lake Ste Claire

Hog Island

Isle au Pêche

Fort Detroit

Ottawa Village

Potawatomi Village

River Rouge

Huron Village

Ecorse River

Turkey Island

Detroit River

Grosse Isle

Bois Blanc

N

MILES

1  0                5

Vicinity of Detroit
·1763·

LAKE ERIE

# Lieut. Jehu Hay's Diary, 1763

*Detroit, May 1, 1763*

THE *1st of May*, Pontiac, the most considerable man in the Ottawa nation, came here with about 50 of his men and told the commandant [Major Henry Gladwin] that in a few days when the rest of his nation came in [from the winter's hunt] he intended to come and make him a formal visit, as is the custom with all the nations once a year. The 7th he came with all the Ottawa and part of several other nations, but we saw from their behavior and from reports[1] that they were not well intentioned; upon which the commandant took such precautions that when they entered the fort (though they were by the nearest accounts about 300 and armed with knives, tomahawks, and a great many with guns cut short and hid under their blankets) they were so much surprised to see our dispositions that they would scarcely sit down to council. However, in about half an hour after they saw that we were prepared for the worst, they sat down and made several

[1] The best evidence points to Angelique Cuillerier as Gladwin's informant about Pontiac's attempted surprise. She told her lover, James Sterling, an Irish trader in the fort, who told Gladwin. Presumably she overheard the chief plotting in her father's house, because Pontiac promised that her father should become commandant of the fort after the Indians drove out the British.

speeches, which were answered as calmly as if we did not suspect them at all, and after receiving some tobacco and bread and some other presents they went away to their camp.

*May 7th* This morning a party sent by him [Pontiac] for that purpose took Capt. Robertson and Sir Robert Davers[2] in a barge near the mouth of Lake Huron, which Capt. Robertson went to sound. They, with part of the boat's crew, were put to death; the rest they took prisoners as we were afterwards informed. The 8th, Pondiac returned with a pipe of peace in order to ask [the] commandant's leave to come next day with his whole nation to bury all bad reports, but the commandant would not give him leave, but told him if he had anything to say he might come with the rest of the chiefs, and he would hear them.

*May 9th* However, instead of coming the 9th, in the afternoon he struck his camp and crossed the river within half a mile of the fort, but being informed by the interpreter that he would not be permitted to come in, he embarked again and he commenced hostilities by killing the King's cattle

[2] Lieut. Charles Robertson was sounding the depth of the St. Clair River for possible ship communication between Detroit and Michilimackinac. Sir Robert Davers was a tourist who had spent a year in Detroit and now was planning a tour of the upper Great Lakes. They and two sailors were killed by the Chippewas, and others in the party taken prisoner.

that were on an island about three miles from the fort, with the people that took care of them and a poor English family that had just built a little house there, as also another English family that lived just behind the fort.[3] He also cut off the communication from the fort to the inhabitants on each side so that we could not get the least thing brought into the fort. He told the inhabitants that the first of them that should bring us any provisions or anything that could be of any service to us, they would put that family to death. They also surrounded the fort and fired a vast number of shots at it and the vessels which were anchored so as to flank the fort both above and below.[4] The garrison lay upon the[ir] arms all night, not being above 120 men, merchants, sick, and officers.[5]

*May 10th* The 10th they surrounded it again and fired very briskly till about 11 or 12 o'clock, when

[3] Disappointed in the failure of his surprise, Pontiac struck at any Englishmen he could find outside the fort. His first victims were a Mrs. Turnbull and two sons in their farm house about a mile from the fort, and the James Fisher family on Belle Isle along with two soldiers acting as herdsmen of the King's cattle. The total was nine deaths.

[4] The two ships were the *Huron*, a schooner, and the *Michigan*, a sloop. They carried supplies and soldiers across Lake Erie between Fort Niagara and Fort Detroit and prevented the siege from being successful.

[5] This statement about the garrison lying on its arms, or the soldiers sleeping on the ramparts (actually the firing platform against the stockade on which they stood in the day time) becomes almost a daily refrain in the diary.

they made some propositions for an accommodation (which was lucky for us, as it gave us time to get provisions into the King's store, as we had not above three weeks' at short allowance). Capt. Campbell and Lieut. McDougall,[6] with the principal part of the French who said they would be answerable for their return, went out to hold council with him, but as soon as Pondiac got them in his possession he changed his mind and would not come to terms, as he had a few hours before promised the French, who seemed to do all in their power to make him disperse his people, but on the contrary sent word to the commandant that he must leave the fort as M. Bellestre[7] did, that was to say to take provision enough with him to carry him to Niagara, but to leave all the merchandise.

To which the commandant answered that he could not come to any terms with him until he sent back Capt. Campbell and Lieut. McDougall, for whom he would give up the two Potawatomies that he had detained for them. The garrison lay on their arms all night as usual. We were at the same time told

[6]Capt. Donald Campbell of the Royal Americans had commanded at Detroit until the arrival of Major Gladwin in 1762 and had gotten along well with the French and the Indians. Lieut. George McDougall, of the same regiment, volunteered to accompany Campbell to the council requested by Pontiac. Like Hay, McDougall married a local French girl, at one time owned Belle Isle, and died in Montreal in 1780.

[7]Mons. Bellestre was the last French commandant at Detroit, who had surrendered the fort to Major Robert Rogers in 1760.

by some French that they thought the best thing we could do would be to save ourselves in the vessels, as there was 1000, some said 1500, Indians ready to fall upon all sides of the fort; but they got for answer that if in case they were three times as numerous there was not an officer or[8]

*May 11th* In the morning Pondiac sent another message desiring the fort to be given up as before, to which the commandant gave an equivocal answer to gain time to get provision, having for two nights before employed some Frenchmen to put some corn and bears' grease on board the vessels, unknown to the Indians. The twelfth in the morning they surrounded the fort and fired upon it and the vessels for about four hours very briskly, though at so great a distance that we had but one man slightly wounded in the fort and another on board one of the vessels. We killed three or four of them, wounded nine or ten. . . .

*May 14th* The fourteenth day they began firing at about eleven o'clock and continued till dark, not daring to approach nearer than the nearest houses that could cover them, which were upwards of two hundred yards off. They fired a great deal but more upon the vessels than on the fort. We had this day a sergeant and one private man wounded. . . .

---

[8] Sentence unfinished, but it shows the bull-headed determination of Major Gladwin. He had been given a fort to hold and he hadn't the slightest intention of giving it up to anyone as long as he remained alive.

*May 22nd*  At 9 o'clock Mr. [Jacques] St. Martin came with a message from the Hurons, who desired him to tell the commandant that they had been forced into the war by the Ottawas . . . to which the commandant desired his interpreter, Mr. St. Martin, to answer . . . they perform their promises and remain quiet, or use their endeavors to separate Pondiac and his followers, who at this time had cut off all communication between us and our outposts, as also lay in wait at different places to intercept all merchants that might be on their way hither. He reigned at this time with most despotic sway over the French, making several of them plow land for him to put corn in the ground, and after they had done would kill their cattle. Three days ago he sent six Frenchmen with some Indians amongst some other nations to advertise them of what he was doing and to bring him word from the Illinois whether what we had told him with regard to the peace was true or not. . . .

*May 24th*  At about seven in the evening the Indians surrounded us and began to fire on the sloop and continued till about ten o'clock, when the people on board observed a great number firing from one place. They pointed a six-pounder and fired it, after which they [the Indians] did not fire ten shots, though they had fired upwards of a thousand before. At eleven they began to fire from Mr. St. Martin's house upon the flag bastion where we are informed there was about two hundred who brought combustibles to set fire to the fort, but none of them dare approach nearer than where they could be covered; they kept a very hot fire till after one which we did not mind, hardly ever returning a shot, till hearing one of them speaking louder than the rest and a great many answering him, the commandant pointed a four-pounder at the place loaded with a ball and grape and fired it, soon after which they went off, not firing twenty shots after it though they had fired very briskly from 11. By the death song that they sang two or three times we imagine there was some killed or wounded. The garrison lay upon the ramparts. . . .

*May 30th* This morning at 8 o'clock we had the disagreeable sight of eight batteaux with provisions that a party of Indians had taken belonging to a party commanded by Lieut. Cuyler the [28th] instant, about 14 miles from the mouth of the [Detroit] River.[9] As the affair happened in the night we have no just accounts of the killed and prisoners, but Lieut. Cuyler with two batteaux made their escape. When they were passing the fort at about 600 yards distance, we called to them, as there was but a few Indians in some of them, and told them to

[9] Unaware of Indian trouble, Lieut. Abraham Cuyler, of the Queen's Rangers, had left Niagara on May 13 with 96 men and 139 barrels of provisions in ten batteaux. His party was attacked at Point Pelée on May 28. Cuyler was wounded, but escaped with 40 men and returned to Niagara. The captured survivors were taken to Detroit and reputedly killed in a drunken victory celebration.

push off towards the vessel and she would cover them with her fire; upon which the foremost, having four soldiers and two Indians in it, put off, the soldiers seizing the Indians and throwing them overboard and gained the vessel, notwithstanding the fire of the Indians from the shore. The batteau had seven barrels of pork and one of flour on board. One of the soldiers fell overboard with the Indian whom, after a great struggle, they tomahawked. . . .

*June 6th* This day we were informed that the commandant of Fort St. Joseph was prisoner with the Potawatomies.[10] We imagine that he was obliged to evacuate his post, not having more than a hundred weight of flour the 12th [of] May, and in attempting to come here was taken. . . .

*June 9th* We were also well assured that the [Fort] Miami[11] was taken, as a Frenchman spoke to the corporal of that garrison who was prisoner with the Indians, who told him that Mr. Holmes had been informed of the designs of the Indians and that he had shut the gates of the fort, which the Indians seeing found they could not take it but by treachery.

[10] Fort St. Joseph was on the St. Joseph River at modern Niles, Mich., under the command of Ens. Francis Schlosser of the 60th regiment.

[11] Fort Miami was at the head of the Maumee River in modern Fort Wayne, Ind. The attackers were some of the local Miamies inspired by the delegation Pontiac had sent to Illinois to solicit help. The commandant was Ens. Robert Holmes of the 60th regiment.

Accordingly they employed a squaw that Mr. Holmes kept to bring him out of the fort to bleed her sister, who was sick in a cabin, and as soon as he came there three or four Ottawas, who had hid themselves on purpose, fired at him and killed him; then took one Welch, whom they had prisoner, and went to the fort and made him tell the men if they would lay down their arms they should be all saved, upon which they opened the gates. We hear they have carried them towards the Illinois. The garrison lay on their arms. . . .

*June 12th* Yesterday and today we buried five corpses that we took up in the river, two of whom we knew, but the rest were so mangled that it was impossible for anybody to have the least knowledge of them. . . .

*June 14th* Yesterday we heard that [Fort] Ouia-tanon[12] was cut off and the garrison taken to the Illinois. Everything quiet today. The garrison lay on the ramparts.

*June 15th* This morning between eleven and twelve o'clock one of the chiefs of the Potawatomies (named Washee) who took St. Joseph's, came with four or five others to change some of their prisoners for the two that we had in custody. After talking near two hours the commandant got them to consent to give Mr. Schlosser and two soldiers that they

[12] Fort Ouiatanon was on the Wabash River just below modern Lafayette, Ind. It was taken by the local Weas again inspired by Pontiac's delegation on its way to Illinois.

brought with them for one of them that he had, and promised them that when they brought the rest of the prisoners he would give them the other. They did not seem to be well contented, as they expected the man of the most consequence in return for the officer, but the commandant was almost sure that if he gave him up they would not give above one of the eleven that remained with them for the other, and therefore detained him.

The account Mr. Schlosser gives of the way he was taken is that about seventeen Potawatomies came into his fort under a pretense of holding a council, after they had engaged the young men of the nation about him to join with them, to whom they promised all the plunder. After they were in the fort, Washee, the Potawatomi chief, went into his room with three or four others, to whom he [Ens. Schlosser] had presented a belt, as he could speak a little of their language himself, for they had detained his interpreter on the other side of the river till everything was ready; but before they had made him an answer a Frenchman came in and told him their design, upon which the cry was given in the fort and they seized him immediately. The young men that [had] agreed to join him [Washee] rushed into the fort, knocking down the sentinel, and before the men could get to their arms put ten of them to death, which Washee tried to prevent but in vain. The remaining three and himself they took prisoners. After this was done, all the chiefs of the St. Joseph

Indians came to Mr. Schlosser and told him that they knew nothing of the affair, that their young men crossed the river in the night unknown to them, and desired him to acquaint the commandant here that they were not concerned in the war, nor would be. . . .

*June 18th* This day the Jesuit[13] arrived from Michilimackinac with the disagreeable news of its being cut off by treachery. The particulars are not yet come to hand. All quiet today. The garrison lay on the ramparts.

*June 19th* This day the Jesuit came into the fort and brought a letter from Capt. [George] Etherington by which we were informed that the 2nd of June the Chippewas were playing at lacrosse at Michilimackinac (three days after they had a council with him and professed a great deal of friendship) . . . and in an instant seized Capt. Etherington and Lieut. [William] Leslye, who were at the gate looking at them playing, forced by the sentry, and entered the fort, where they found their squaws (who had been previously placed with their tomahawks) with which they forced the guard before they could get under arms, killed thirteen men on the spot with Lieut. Jamet, who fought with his sword against five for a long time, but after receiving thirty-six wounds fell in their hands, after which they cut off

[13]Father Pierre du Jaunay had been missionary to the Ottawas in northern Michigan since 1735. He died at Quebec in 1780.

his head and killed six of their prisoners.[14] They pillaged all the merchants and got fifty barrels of powder with lead in proportion. The Ottawas took the officers and eleven of their prisoners from them whom they keep at the priest's house. . . .

*June 26th* [Sunday] This day Pondiac went to mass on the other side of the river, and after it was over he took three chairs that belonged to the people for himself and his guard to ride in to look for provision, making the French his chair men. He gave billets to the people for their cattle signed with his mark, with the imitation of a coon drawn on the top of each billet. . . .

*June 29th* This day we heard that the Indians that went from this [place] about twenty days ago had taken [Fort] Presqu'Isle,[15] that they lost three men

[14]The Chippewas seized Fort Michilimackinac, at modern Mackinaw City, Mich., on June 2 by arranging a game of lacrosse on the beach. When one of the players lobbed the ball over the stockade, the Indians rushed into the fort ostensibly to retrieve it, but dropped their sticks, took tomahawks and guns from their robed squaws, and began killing the soldiers. Twenty soldiers and one trader were killed, along with Lieut. John Jamet, and the others taken prisoner. The local Ottawas, jealous of having been left out of the plot, intervened to protect the prisoners and insisted on their being carried to Montreal for ransom.

[15]Fort Presqu'Isle (Erie, Pa.) was taken on June 22 by the detachment of 200 Ottawas, Hurons, and Chippewas sent from Detroit by Pontiac and a contingent of Senecas who had already taken Fort Venango (Franklin, Pa.) and Fort Le Boeuf (Waterford, Pa.) after they heard the western Indians were in revolt. Ens. John Christie, the commandant at Presqu'Isle, was brought to Detroit by the Hurons and delivered over to Gladwin on July 9.

there, that the way they took it was by setting fire to a small house that was close to the fort and which communicated the fire to it, that they killed but three, and the officer with several prisoners were given to the nations near that place. . . .

*June 30th* At 12 o'clock the wind sprang up favorably for the schooner, when she weighed anchor and reached this about 3, with a detachment of 22 men from the 80th regiment, and Lieut. Cuyler and 28 men of Capt. Hopkins' company of Rangers, with 150 barrels of provision and some ammunition. Lieut. Cuyler informs us that Presqu'Isle was burned the 22nd instant [June] after being attacked three days. . . .

*July 2nd* At three o'clock this morning Lieut. McDougall with an Albany trader arrived at the fort, having made their escape from the Indians . . .

This morning Mr. [Pierre] Labutte came into the fort and informed us that as soon as the Chippewas were informed that we had killed the son of their great chief, they went to Pondiac and told him that he was the cause of all their ill luck, that he caused them to enter into the war and did nothing himself, that he was very brave in taking a loaf of bread or a beef from a Frenchman who made no resistance, but it was them that had all the men killed and wounded every day. For that reason they would take that from him which he intended to save himself by in the end; then went and took Capt. Campbell, stripped him, and carried him to their camp, where they killed him, took out his heart and ate it reeking from his body, cut off his head, and the rest of the body they divided into small pieces. . . .

*July 6th* At 12 o'clock the commandant sent the sloop up to Pondiac's camp under the command of Capt. Hopkins[16] and Ensign Pauli,[17] but the wind being very weak they [the Ottawas] had time to remove almost all their things out of their cabins and send their women and children away before she arrived. However, they fired near fifty cannon at those that were there and threw several shells among them. We have not heard what number was killed or wounded. . . .

*July 10th* Last night at twelve o'clock the enemy made a large float with four batteaux, which they filled with fagots, birch bark, and tar and other combustibles, which they brought into the middle of the stream about a half a mile above the vessels and set on fire; but the vessels being properly moored let go one of their cables and sheered off from it, letting it pass at about 150 yards distance. This we suppose was not entirely the invention and work of Indians. . . .

[16] Capt. Joseph Hopkins of Maryland had obtained a commission in the Queen's Rangers when it was organized in 1762. He was an extremely capable officer, always volunteering for hazardous duty.

[17] Ens. Christopher Pauli was the commandant of Fort Sandusky, on Sandusky Bay, before it was taken on May 16 by Ottawas and Hurons. He was the only survivor of the garrison and had escaped from the Indians and entered Fort Detroit on July 3.

*July 11th* This night and between 12 and one o'-clock the Indians sent down another large fire float which passed without doing any damage. They had made two, but Capt. Hopkins, who was on board the sloop, fired a cannon at them as soon as he perceived the first and frightened them so that they jumped out of their canoes and let the other go without being lighted, which we towed on shore. The garrison lay on the ramparts. . . .

*July 28th* This day we were informed by Mr. Sterling that Mademoiselle Cuillerier told him that Godfroy told Pondiac when he returned from the Illinois that he [the French commandant] could not send him any succour yet, as they had heard by a Spanish vessel that peace was made; but that as soon as his couriers arrived that he had sent to New Orleans, if he found the news to be false, he would see what he could do, and desired that the inhabitants should not appear in it at all, but keep themselves quiet. . . .

*July 29th* This morning at half past four o'clock, it being very foggy, we heard the report of several muskets and now and then, as we thought, swivels at the Huron village, which we [thought] to be some Indians firing at the schooner, as she might have come that far up the river without our seeing her in the night. But in about half an hour to our great surprise we saw about twenty batteaux, which upon their coming near we found to be English boats with a detachment of about 260 men under the command of Capt. Dalyell.[18] They came the south side of the Lake [Erie] and burned a small Indian village near Sandusky that the Indians had abandoned. They had fourteen men wounded in passing the Huron village. . . .

*July 31st* This morning at three quarters after two a detachment of 247 men under the command of Capt. Dalyell marched out with an intention to surprise the Indian camp about three miles and a half from the fort.

But whether the enemy were informed of it or discovered them in marching out is not known, but when they were within a half mile of their camp they were fired upon by a great number of Indians from behind orchards, fences, and entrenchments that they had posted themselves in for that purpose, which put them [the soldiers] a little in confusion at first, but they soon recovered their disorder and forced the enemy from their lodgements. They then finding that their scheme could not be put in execution, they thought of making the best retreat they could, the enemy being twice as numerous as they

[18] This detachment under Capt. James Dalyell had been sent by Gen. Amherst. Both officers expected that it would enable Gladwin to break the siege and defeat the Indians. Gladwin knew this was not possible, but Dalyell, arguing persistently and implying that Amherst expected some offensive move, persuaded Gladwin to let him lead a sortie. With him went regulars of the 55th, 60th, and 80th regiments and some New York provincials under Major Robert Rogers, who should have been allowed to plan and lead the whole expedition. As it was he had to save it in the end.

were. Knowing they could not expect any more succour from the garrison, for which purpose they took post in several houses that were most advantageous to prevent the enemy as much as possible from getting between them and the fort. Capt. Dalyell, who behaved with all the bravery in the world, was unluckily killed. After receiving the fire from the enemy, though Capt. Grant begged of him either to push on immediately [or] make a retreat without loss of time, he remained almost in the same place for at least three-quarters of an hour, soon after which he was killed; and Capt. Grant then with the assistance of the two row galleys made as good a retreat as was possible for anybody to do, after sending off all the wounded and all the dead except seven.

We lost in this affair Capt. Dalyell killed, Capt. [Robert] Gray, Lieut. [John] Luke and Lieut. [Archibald] Brown of the 55th wounded, one sergeant and 13 rank and file killed, and one drummer and 25 wounded. 60th regiment: one private and seven wounded. 80th regiment: two killed and three wounded. Q. A. Rangers: two killed and one wounded, and a trader's servant wounded. Total, officers included, killed and wounded: 61.[19] The Indians say they had five killed and eleven wounded. . . .

[19] Actual casualties were 23 killed, 39 wounded, and an unknown number taken prisoner—better than 25% of the force.

*Aug. 7th* This day the commandant received a letter from Capt. Etherington dated at Michilimackinac the 18th July, who with his garrison and that of Fort Edward Augustus[20] was then going into the boats to go to Montreal, as also all the English merchants. . . .

*Sept. 4th* Last night at about 9 o'clock, 340 Indians embarked in canoes and went to board the schooner. The merchants were on shore. The channel where the vessel lay not being very wide, and rushes growing on each side of it, they came within a little more than a hundred yards of her before they were discovered and then rushed in at once upon her, surrounding her with canoes and batteaux and under a very brisk fire attempted to cut holes in her stern and the cable. The cable they cut, but notwithstanding there was but twelve on board, two of whom, Mr. Horsey and another, was killed and four wounded at the beginning, they never was able to board her, but obliged to fly with the loss (as the French tell us) of eight killed and twenty wounded. . . .

*Sept. 5th* At 11 the wind sprang up a little and the schooner came in sight, and at half past three cast anchor opposite the fort. She brought 47 barrels of flour and 160 of pork.

*Oct. 2nd* This morning at 10 o'clock Lieut. [Dietrich] Brehm, Lieut. [Edward] Abbott, Ens. Riggell, and myself were sent up the river in four

[20] Indians had forced the abandonment of Fort Edward Augustus at Green Bay, Wis., on June 21.

armed batteaux to reconnoitre an island in the mouth of Lake St. Clair to see if it was possible to bring wood from it for the garrison, and to try to bring off a ship's boat that the Indians took from Capt. Robertson. When we were about four miles from the fort, the Indians began to fire upon us from holes they had made on the side of the river, and two or three times attempted to put off in a batteau and two or three canoes, as we imagined, to cross the river to fire upon us from each shore, but we drove them ashore as soon as they were well on board. But at last seeing we only lost time with them, [we] pushed on to perform what we were sent about.

When we had gained the upper end of Hog Island[21] we saw them push off with nineteen canoes and batteaux and seemed to follow us, and when we were in the narrow part of the river [they] surrounded us under a brisk fire from each shore; upon which we turned to attack them, they still pushing on with great bravery all open to our fire, making a great hallooing. At length Lieut. Brehm got a good shot at some of them with a four-pounder charged with grape at about forty or fifty yards distance, which so disabled [them] that out of about 15 or 16 that were in it we could not see but two that paddled. They then put on shore, some on one side of the river and some on the other, and cried two death halloos. We then rowed up and down in the same

[21] Hog Island was the name of modern Belle Isle.

part of the river and called to them to put off again, that we were waiting for them. But they were then very quiet and did not halloo as in the beginning and chose rather to fire [a] few straggling shots from shore than attempt coming off again. Then finding it too late to proceed, we returned to the fort. We had one man killed and three wounded, two of which were very slight. We have not yet heard what number of them were killed or wounded. Upon our return we were informed that one of the vessels was in the mouth of the river.

*Oct. 3rd* At 12 o'clock, the wind being almost south, heard firing of cannon and small arms down the river, and at one or half past the schooner came in sight. About half past three she arrived at the fort, in which came Capt. Montresor, who informed us that the sloop was lost the 28th of August between Presqu'Isle and Niagara;[22] the provision and guns were all lost except 185 barrels which they brought in the schooner. The rigging was all carried to Niagara. . . .

*Oct. 19th* The councils that have been held these few days past have been attended with this good effect: that we have been able to get in some wheat and some little [corn] flour, without which we should not have an ounce of flour in the garrison

[22]Loss of the sloop left only the schooner to maintain communication between Detroit and Niagara. Capt. John Montresor, noted army engineer and cartographer, made a manuscript map in color of the Detroit River at this time which is in the Clements Library.

ten days past, as the men for upwards of seven weeks past have had only five pounds of flour per week and for the other two pounds [they received] half a gallon of wheat each. . . .

*Oct. 30th* Last night Mons. Dequindre, a cadet, arrived from the Illinois and was in council with Pondiac and the chiefs of all the nations here, and this morning brought a letter to the commandant from Mons. de Neyon,[23] commandant of the Illinois country, with a speech which he sent addressed to all Indians with three belts of wampum and four pipes of peace which he distributed to the nations as he came along. In the speech he let them know that peace was made between England and France and exhorted them to live in peace with us, telling them that fighting against us at present was fighting against them, and desiring them to esteem their brothers the French that remained amongst us, as they would never be abandoned by them. That they [the French] changed their situation as the King ordered and that they had given up those parts of the country that belonged to the King and not theirs, and desired an answer to his speech telling them [the Indians] they should always receive succour from them at such and such places. That their villages would be full of ammunition and merchandise.

[23] Major Neyon de Villiers, French commandant of Fort de Chartres, was telling Pondiac that he could not send any military aid, and telling the French inhabitants to stay clear of the conflict between the Indians and the English.

Upon which Pondiac sent in word to the commandant that their hatchet was buried and desired to have his answer in writing. To which the commandant answered that if he had begun the war it would be in his power to end it; but as it was him [Pontiac], he must wait the pleasure of the general, to whom he would write and inform him of his [Pontiac's] pacific inclination, in case he committed no more hostilities. Pondiac then said he would not commit any more and would come when he was sent for. . . .

*Nov. 11th* At three o'clock the schooner arrived, in which came Mr. Willyamos of the 80th who brought us the disagreeable account of a party of about 70 men being cut off at the carrying place at Niagara[24] by a large body of Indians, as also the loss of most of the carriages and bullocks, which undoubtedly prevented the army from coming so soon as they otherwise would have done.

This morning two Indians arrived from Pointe aux Pins with a letter, one half wrote in Erse[25] and the other in English, from Major Moncrieffe giving an account of the batteaux being cast away the 7th instant at the Highlands, beyond the said Pointe, where they lost 20 boats and 50 barrels of provisions,

[24] Actually 72 men were slaughtered on Sept. 14 by the Senecas in an ambush on the portage trail from Fort Niagara, at the mouth of the river, and Fort Schlosser, at the top of the falls and two miles from the dock for Lake Erie vessels. The news was brought by Lieut. Samuel Willyamos.

[25] The Scottish Gaelic language.

with two officers and a surgeon drowned, as also 70 men;[26] and that all their ammunition, even the men's cartridges, were wet, and that they had wisely (not knowing our circumstances) taken a resolution to turn back to Niagara.

But from the steps Major Gladwin had taken some time before he was in a situation to keep a tolerable garrison[27] here with provision till the month of May, and was in a good way of getting enough till the month of July, though at the expense of listening to the demands of peace the Indians had some time before made, which notwithstanding he did not grant them. . . .

[26] Major Thomas Moncrieffe reported the loss in a storm on Nov. 7 of 70 men and 20 boats from a reinforcement of 600 commanded by Major John Wilkins. The officers decided to turn back to Niagara. This reinforcement was intended to enable Gladwin to punish the Indians around Detroit.

[27] Although it is not recorded in Hay's diary, Gladwin sent back east 243 officers and men on Nov. 20, because he could not feed them during the winter.

# 8

## Journal of Lord Adam Gordon

*

*How Our Cities Looked*
1765

# How Our Cities Looked
## 1765

*Often the best view of colonial America was sup-*
*plied by foreign visitors. Not only were they gen-*
*erally objective and intelligent, but in making a*
*tour they could offer comparisons among cities and*
*regions. One of the best descriptive accounts of*
*America before the Revolution—and least known—*
*is the personal narrative of Lord Adam Gordon*
*in 1765.*

*Gordon was the fourth son of the second Duke of*
*Gordon, a Scot. He was born about 1725–26 and*
*entered the army as an ensign in 1746. He also*
*served in Parliament as a member for Aberdeen-*
*shire, 1754–68, and for Kincardineshire, 1774–88.*
*In 1762 he was made colonel of the 66th Regiment*
*of foot, which he took out to Jamaica two years later.*
*Late in 1764, having some time available, he began*
*a tour of the American mainland at Florida. Pro-*
*ceeding northward up the Atlantic seaboard, he*
*commented on military installations, crops and*
*agricultural potential, cities, inhabitants, and*
*customs. From New York City he moved up to*
*Albany, then west to Niagara Falls. Turning*
*northeast he crossed Lake Ontario and descended*

*the St. Lawrence as far as Quebec. He moved south-ward along Lake Champlain, returned to Albany, then dipped into Massachusetts and Connecticut on his way to Boston. His final journey took him to Rhode Island and through Long Island Sound to New York again, where he took ship to England in October 1765.*

*Lord Gordon married but had no issue. He be-came commander of the forces in Scotland in 1782 and retired in 1798. His manuscript journal is among the King's manuscripts in the British Museum, and a transcript is in the Library of Congress. It is entitled "Journal of an Officer in the West Indies who Travelled over a Part of the West Indies and of North America." It was first printed in* Travels in the American Colonies, *New York, 1916, edited by Newton D. Mereness. Not all of the journal is reprinted here, as his sojourn in the West Indies has been omitted and some pieces of military description no longer have interest.*

*Gordon was neither a supercilious aristocrat amused by the foibles of inferior colonials nor a partisan enthusiast for democratic home rule. He was traveling through the colonies at the time the Stamp Act was being debated. This tax had been proposed in 1764 and was enacted by Parliament in January 1765 to take effect on November 1. Gordon thought it eminently proper that the colo-*

nists should help pay the cost of their defense, but he was not belligerent about it. Indeed, when he reached Boston a committee headed by James Otis waited on him with an official welcome and a request that after he returned home he represent to Parliament the uneasiness and opposition of Massachusetts over the new act. Gordon replied that he would always exert himself "where the interests of Great Britain and America are concerned, which to me seem inseparable." It was a nice evasion of commitment to repeal of the tax. When he sailed from New York, the Stamp Act Congress, called to resist the act, was in session.

In his journal Gordon reveals a natural predilection to notice military structures and recall battles, but he also shows himself to have a farmer's eye as he examined soil, drainage, crops, and fertilizers. He was impressed by American towns and cities, each one appearing more attractive to him than the last. In general he liked the people, too. Of course, he was well received wherever he stopped, because of his personal qualities, his political office, and his title. His journal was hurriedly written, with long involved sentences, uncertain antecedents, excessive punctuation, and inconsistencies of style. Without adding words, we have tried to edit his narrative to be more easily understood by a modern reader.

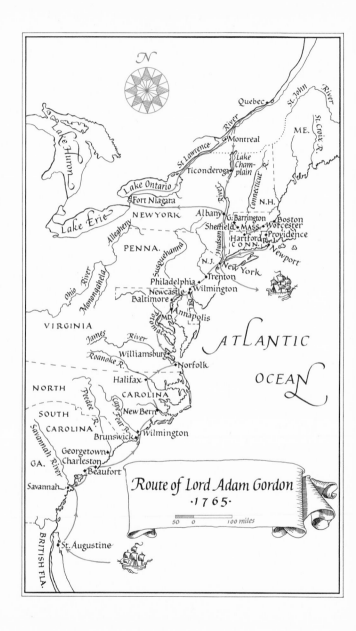

Route of Lord Adam Gordon
·1765·

50  0  100 miles

# Journal of Lord Adam Gordon

ABOUT noon we came to an anchor off [St.] Augustine bar, in about five fathom water; the island on which the town stands, as well as the island on which the lighthouse is built, being then in sight. The pilot boat, and a very ill-calculated insufficient boat she is, came off and carried us in over the bar and breakers. In this short passage, I apprehend, we ran more risk of being lost than in any former part of our voyage. . . .

Augustine has all the appearance of a place that will thrive, although the bar is an insurmountable obstacle to its being a place of exportation; for at the best of tide you can bring with you but twelve feet of water, yet when once in the harbor you are safe and have deep water. But large ships lying at anchor off the bar, or plying off and on, run risk of being blown on shore, or on the breakers which are terrible, and what is worst it shall happen in blowing weather that for days and weeks no boat or small vessel can venture either to go out or in over the bar. As soon as the projected road from the Province of Georgia to Augustine is completed, most people will come that way to Augustine from Savannah, Charleston, and all the northern provinces.

It may not be improper here to take notice that the River St. Mary's, which divides Georgia from East Florida, may in time become a useful port to both provinces. . . . The land on both banks of this very remarkable river is mostly pine barren, with here and there some trifling swamps and several fine bluffs, particularly on the Florida shore of it. . . .

On the opposite side of East Florida [peninsula] and about half [the] distance from St. Mark's to the cape of Florida, lies the Bay of Tampa, which is sometimes called *Bahia del Spiritu Santo*. It is supposed to have water to carry in any ship in the world, and safe space within to contain any fleet, but as an exact survey of it is now actually taking, by orders from home, I will say no more of it. . . . The land for thirty miles round this bay is claimed by John Gordon, Esq.[1] as a Spanish purchase. Two considerable rivers empty themselves into it, the heads of which (some imagine) actually [connect] with the rivers that fall into the sea near Augustine, but most people allow that with a very moderate expense a water communication could be made so as to have inland navigation across that part of East Florida lying in a line from Augustine to the Bay of Appalachi, or near it.[2]

The fort at Augustine is a quarré,[3] smaller but better finished than the fort at Mobile. It is built of

[1] John Gordon (d. 1778), a Charleston merchant, claimed he had purchased from departing Spaniards several hundred thousand acres of land in 1763. He carried on a fruitless campaign to obtain English recognition of his title.

[2] This idea of an inland canal crossing the northern portion of the state is still very much alive. A small portion has been completed, the alarms of ecologists and conservationists have been studied, and work continues on a two-century-old idea.

[3] Quarré, a favorite word with Gordon, was simply a square.

stone which, soft at first quarrying, grows hard in the weather and is extremely white. It is casemated all round the four sides and can mount from seventy to eighty pieces of cannon. At present no more than twenty are mounted. It is neatly executed, but on too small a scale, though strong on account of the great difficulty of approaching it, owing to the swampy land and very shoal water that almost surrounds it.

Governor [James] Grant has fitted up the house and formed his establishment, his council and courts. Many gentlemen of worth and substance from Carolina and Georgia are in terms to settle in this province and intend to plant indigo,[4] rice, and cotton, all of which it is presumed must answer well. Towards the cape and on the south keys grow abundance of mahogany, live oak, and other timber valuable in ship building and other uses; the rivers, bays, and coasts abound in fish, more and in greater variety than in Europe. The inhabitants of [New] Providence[5] catch turtle there every year and supply themselves and the adjacent continent with it, as they do Europe with mahogany cut on the above named keys. Two hundred Bermudians have intentions to settle themselves towards the cape next fall and more of them will follow, since they are assisted and enabled by a generous and public-spirited do-

[4] Blue dye used to be extracted from this plant. Since indigo dyes now are made synthetically, the word has come to mean various blue vat dyes.

[5] New Providence, in the Bahama Islands, east of Florida.

nation of £5 sterling to each settler, woman and child, by John Savage, Esq. of Charleston, who means to lay out for this purpose not less than £5000 sterling.

The soil in and near Augustine is light and sandy, yet it produces every species of garden stuff known in Britain when sown in due season. When I was there in November [1764] we had peas, beans, salad, oranges, limes, critons,[6] and lemons; the gardens of every house in town are full of them and also produce grapes, figs (two crops), peaches, and pomegranates. I am assured the avocado pear, the plantain,[7] and other West India fruits have come to perfection there; from whence one may suppose it is not impracticable (particularly towards the cape, where there is richer land and more sun) to raise sugar, coffee, pimento, and all the West India productions.

The town of Augustine has several good houses in it, the streets are not ill-laid out, but too narrow (a Spanish mode). It is remarkably healthy, perhaps the most so of any town in America; the climate in winter is pleasant beyond the idea of any man who has never been out of Europe. The Spaniards lived in it to a remarkable old age, healthy and cheerful; our sick soldiers from the Havana almost all did well and continue to look well in Augustine, and although

[6] Probably citrons; a fruit that resembles a lemon but is larger.

[7] Similar to a banana, but larger, starchier, less sweet, and greenish in color.

surrounded with water, meadow, and marsh, fevers and agues are scarce known. It is enclosed by a line and a sort of ditch; the line was planted with the palmetto royal, but its best defense is the great difficulty to bring up any artillery against it, for the reasons already given. After all, from what I have seen of it and heard of it, was I ever to apply for any land in America, it should be in this province, which has many of the advantages and none of the disagreeable circumstances that too visibly must occur in planting and settling the adjacent Province of West Florida.

On Thursday the 28th of November I crossed the swatch[8] and got on board the packet, and on the 2nd of December after a rather tedious passage we came into Tybee road, which is the entrance into Savannah River, passed three miles higher up, and came to an anchor off of Cockspur Fort on the right hand going up.

The Province of Georgia extends from St. Mary's to the east bank of the Savannah River, the northern stream of which divides it from South Carolina. It was settled originally by [James] Oglethorpe in 1733 and was vested in the hands of several trustees. However, that plan failed and for a little more than twelve years it has been a royal government, since which alteration it has annually increased and in a great proportion, too. So late as the year 1761 the

[8]Open sea or an open channel, in this instance between the shore and an off-shore boat.

rice exported from this province did not exceed 5000 barrels; in 1763 it amounted to 12,000 and is annually increasing. In this same year they exported commodities to the amount of £50,000 sterling.

The capital town, called Savannah, is extremely well laid out, and the buildings in it are increasing in number and size. It stands on a bluff fifty feet above the surface of the river, about 15 miles from the mouth at Tybee lighthouse, about [22] miles below Purrysburg [South Carolina] and near 300 miles below Augusta, to which place Savannah River is navigable for large boats. By land the distance is near half as much.

Within twelve miles of Savannah the Governor [James Wright] carried me to visit the orphan house, which is a large substantial commodious building erected by contributions collected from the charitable and benevolent by the Rev. Mr. George Whitefield, and supported to this period in the same manner.[9] Several orphans have been reared and educated here and put out to different masters.

[9] Whitefield first raised money in England for an orphanage in Georgia and obtained a grant of land from the trustees of the colony in 1739. It was established in Bethesda and supported by money Whitefield solicited in his preaching tours through America. If it seems odd to find an orphanage in the newest and least populated colony, Benjamin Franklin explained the reason for it: the colonists sent to Georgia by the trustees were unfit to endure the hardships of making a settlement and died in large numbers, leaving many children unprovided for.

Upwards of £12,000 sterling has by the books been collected, expended, and most exactly accounted for by the said reverend gentleman, who has contributed a sum little short of £3000 of his own towards it and is now about conveying and punctually vesting it (together with all the land, Negroes, stock, etc. amounting to an annual fund of near £500 a year sterling) in the hands of trustees, to be named by royal charter, for a college to educate youth, which disinterested plan is just[ly] much applauded by the Governor and Province of Georgia as tending very much to the advantage of that province, and all other [of] His Majesty's southern dominions, where no place for education of that kind has yet been attempted.

The produce of silk does well here, but will stand in need of the aiding hand of Parliament. The annual quantity, at an average of three years past, made and sent to Britain has been about 1000 pounds weight and is likely rather to increase than diminish. Mulberry trees grow in great perfection, as well as other European productions, except apples. I saw a cabbage from one root which produced many heads and spread over a circumference of thirty feet. It has stood and seeded three years. The same garden produced a potato which weighed ten pounds and three-quarters.

The governor and council live all in love and unanimity, and there is all the probability in the world, to judge from the face of the land, the multitude and depth as well as the long course of their rivers, their inshore navigation, and the security derived to them from the addition of the two new southern provinces, as well as their own industry and application, that Georgia will become one of the richest and most considerable provinces of British America, and that in a very few years provided peace continues.

The soil about Savannah is light and sandy, which is troublesome in windy weather; the tide land on both sides the river is mostly cypress swamp and the fittest for rice and all other productions that can exist, since when properly banked in and drained you need have no dependence on seasons, but either overflow or keep dry your fields, just as you please. . . . The exports from Georgia are rice, indigo, pitch, tar, turpentine, hides, deerskins, timber of most kinds and for most purposes, and raw silk. I am told Sunbury is a thriving place and a tolerable harbor and bar; a forty-gun ship can come up above Tybee and lie safe. . . .

I arrived at Charleston, the metropolis of South Carolina, on the 8th of December, 1764, having landed at Beaufort, in Port Royal Island, some days before from Savannah River. . . . It is of all the southern provinces the most considerable, on account of the number of inhabitants, the quantity and variety of its productions and exports, and the good condition of its inhabitants. There seems in general to be but two classes of people: the planters who are the proprietors, and the merchants who purchase and ship the produce.

Rice and indigo are the two grand staples of this province, of which very great quantities are annually made and exported to Europe and elsewhere. It has been augmenting annually in numbers, wealth, and industry since the Crown purchased out the lords proprietors, and as none of its exports or productions interfere with those of the mother country it will be prudent in her to give this province all possible encouragement.

Almost every family of note has a town residence to which they repair on public occasions and generally for the three sickly months in the fall, it being a certainty that the town of Charleston is at present the most healthy spot in the province; fevers and other disorders are both less frequent in it and less virulent in their symptoms. This is attributed to the air being mended by the number of fires in town as much as to its cool situation on a point at the junction of the two navigable streams, called Ashley and Cooper Rivers.

The inhabitants are courteous, polite, and affable, the most hospitable and attentive to strangers of any I have yet seen in America, very clever in business, and almost all of them, first or last, have made a trip to the mother country. It is the fashion, indeed, to send home all their children for education, and and if it was not owing to the nature of their estates in this province, which they keep all in their own

*Charleston, South Carolina*
From *The London Magazine*, June 1762

hands and require the immediate overlooking of the proprietor, I am of opinion the most opulent planters would prefer a home life. It is in general believed that they are more attached to the mother country than those provinces which lie more to the northward, and which having hardly any staple commodities of their own growth, except lumber, stock, and horses, depend mostly on smuggling molasses and other contraband commodities.

The town of Charleston is very pleasantly seated at the conflux of two pretty rivers from which all the country produce is brought down and in return all imported goods are sent up the country. The streets are straight, broad, and airy, the churches are handsome, the other places of worship are commodious, and many of the houses belonging to individuals are large and handsome, having all the conveniences one sees at home. There is a law against building houses of wood, which like other laws in other countries nobody observes; however, the most considerable buildings are of brick, the others of cypress and yellow pine. The houses now are about fifteen hundred, but increase annually in a very surprising manner.

Their bar, which is very intricate, seems their only defense, for though they have a fort below the town, and a kind of earthen rampart with some tabby[10] works round particular parts of Charleston, yet it

---

[10] Tabby was a masonry made of lime, shells or gravel, and water.

would not be tenable against attacks of shipping or from the land, and therefore must fall a prey to any enemy the moment we lose our superiority at sea. A forty-gun ship has been in, but small frigates and sloops are generally employed on that station.

The town of Beaufort, situated on Port Royal Island and Sound, has more depth of water on its bar, but being on an island there is a difficulty of bringing down the exportable commodities, which will forever prevent its rivaling Charleston in wealth or grandeur.

On the northern part of South Carolina stands Georgetown, a pretty little town near Winyah River and not far from Pedee, Black River, and Waccamaw, which river I should think would make a more sure and commodious boundary between the two Carolinas than any limits they now have.

The back country towards the Cherokee Mount-[ain]s and nation is all healthy and fertile land, producing large oak and other deciduous timber, and is finely watered without much sand or pine barren, but is not yet fully peopled. In general what part of South Carolina is planted is counted unhealthy, owing to the rice dams and swamps which as they occasion a great quantity of stagnated water in summer never fail to increase the number of insects and to produce the fall fevers and agues, dry gripes, and other disorders which are often fatal to the lower set of people, as well white as black.

Within these two or three last years a pretty considerable quantity of flax and hemp has been raised by the Germans and other back settlers, which as well as the produce of a considerable part of North Carolina comes down to Charleston in wagons drawn with four horses, two abreast, perhaps at the distance of 300 miles. This would appear extraordinary at home, but it must be remembered that they live at no more expense when traveling than they would at home, since they lie in the woods all night, make a good fire to dress their bacon, and turn their horses loose near them till daylight, after which they proceed on their journey and carry back in return what goods they stand in need of themselves or for their neighbors in the back settlements.

It is pretty singular to remark that the number of white inhabitants fit to bear arms, in one of their back counties called Craven County, does at present exceed what was the number of fighting men in all the province seven years ago. From this I conclude that the farther you go back from the seaboard in America, the more fertile the land is and the more healthy the climate, for there the people increase and breed and rear up more children than towards the pine barren and sandy shores.

The tide swampland in these southern provinces is by much the most valuable, since when they are properly banked in and your trunks and dams in perfect good order, by a judicious use of these advantages it is alternately equally capable and fit to produce the two great staple commodities—viz. rice and indigo; the first requiring an uncommon degree of moisture or water, and the last, dry and rich land, although the light land very near the shore will fetch very surprising crops of indigo for two or three years, but it must then be thrown out and left to time to recover its fertility.

Poultry and pork, particularly hams, are excellent here; beef and mutton middling, and fish very rare and dear. The general drink of the better people is punch and Madeira wine, and many prefer grog and toddy. All the poor and many of the rich eat rice for bread and give it even a preference; they use it in their cakes, called journey cakes, and boiled, or else boiled Indian corn which they call hominy, and of this they have two sorts, the great and small, the last I think the best.

Upon the whole, this is undoubtedly one of the most opulent and most increasing colonies in America, and bids fair to exceed all the others if it advances in the like proportion as it has done for forty years past. The unhappy differences which have subsisted for some years past between the Governor and the Commons House of Assembly, and are not yet set to rights, have been the means of this country not standing so well at home as otherwise they would have done and as they really deserve to do.

The country from Pedee River to Brunswick in North Carolina is altogether a pine barren, as indeed is most of that province that lies on the seaboard, but up Cape Fear River, after it divides into the Northeast and Northwest Rivers, the land grows better and when properly cleared and cultivated will produce all manner of grain in plenty and perfection.

About twelve miles below Brunswick lies Fort Johnston, a tolerable little quarré built of tabby and mounting about thirty pieces of cannon, 18 and 9-pounders. The best of the water lies near this fort, though there is another channel for small vessels. The bar is not a bad one and has on it about 19 feet or better at high water.

About fifteen miles above Brunswick, on the forks of the river, lies the town of Wilmington, a very pretty situation, but the land about is very poor. Near it is a good sawmill and a very commodious creek. The country from Wilmington to New Bern is very different, but about New Bern, on the conflux of the Neuse and the Trent, the land is better and if the seat of government should ever happen to be established there, as it probably may from its being nearly central, it will become a place of note very soon and will outvie any other town in North Carolina. From that to Tar River, Roanoke River, and Halifax the country mends as one goes back; near the last place at Occaneechy Neck there is an excellent tract of land; on it is the seat of Mr. [Willie] Jones,[11] a good house and a pretty place. From that you have but a few miles to the Virginia line.

[11] Willie Jones (*c.* 1741–1801) of Halifax, N. C., was an aide to Gov. Tryon, but became a rebel political leader in the Revolution.

The Province of North Carolina abounds in white inhabitants; they are said to be upwards of 42,000 men fit to bear arms and live mostly in the back country. They grow but very little rice or indigo, raise a good deal of wheat and other grain, and export more naval stores, pitch, and tar than any other province, also some deerskins and other furs, but they are much divided among themselves. Mr. Dobbs, their governor, died whilst I was there and is succeeded by Colonel William Tryon, a very worthy gentleman, very agreeable to the province, and equal in every respect to the charge His Majesty has reposed in him. . . .

Brunswick does not seem very thriving, although the late and the present governors have mostly made it their residence. Wilmington is a larger and more populous town than Brunswick. It lies up the same river 15 miles which, close to it, forks and runs in both divisions for two hundred miles up and more. On these branches I saw some good provision land and some swamp, which if well managed would bring rice; but the rice produced in that province falls short of that in South Carolina, being less heavy in equal quantities. Hitherto the settlers have gone more upon naval stores than raising crops, and in that and cutting lumber and staves consist most their sure trade. Here in the back lands they raise hemp, flax, wheat, corn, and peas, and are extremely populous in whites, who come out poor and earn with hard labor their bread and clothing.

It is far behind the neighboring provinces in industry and application. My Lord Granville is proprietor of more than one-half of the best of the province and though it is but an unprofitable estate to his lordship, it affects the whole and is the means of differences and disputes, which hurt the whole. Mr. Dobbs and the Assembly could not agree for some years past, but I [have] reason to believe that Mr. Tryon, the present lieutenant governor, by his prudence and coolness and by siding with no party, but doing the King's business and consulting the good of the whole and moving the Assembly to New Bern, the most central town, will greatly reconcile the heats and animosities which have long subsisted between the northern and southern interests of this province. . . .

After you cross James River the land mends and is good all the way to Williamsburg, which is the seat of government [of Virginia] and much resembles a good country town in England. Here is a very handsome statehouse, commodious for all the courts and both the Houses of Council and Assembly, a very large and handsome college [with] probably eighty students, a foundation of Mr. Boyle's for the education of six Indian boys. One Mr. [James] Horrocks is president and there are two other masters. There are many good houses in town, where the courts meet twice a year, in April and October, and continue for 24 days together, except Sundays. The people are well bred, polite, and extremely civil to strangers.

The Governor's house is handsome and commodious, and he himself very happy and the people so in him.[12]

The Governor and Council are judges in all causes. There are two other courts of oyer and terminer[13] at which the Council also attend; their powers are greater than those of any other province and they have no chief justice.

The principal rivers of this province, beginning to the southward, are James, York, Rappahannock, and Potomac, which divides [it] from Maryland. These fork and form several large and navigable rivers which go up the country, some of them two hundred, and some of them more, miles.

I am well assured by gentlemen whose veracity I can depend upon that the back country of Virginia, particularly towards Lord Fairfax's property, is as fine and rich land as any in the world, producing all kinds of grain and grass in perfection and great abundance, being also extremely temperate as to climate and having scarce any mosquitoes or other troublesome insects. The soil of the lower part of Virginia is light, though often a whitish clay at bottom, producing the best tobacco in the world and

[12] Francis Fauquier was the governor in residence, but legally the lieutenant governor. Sir Jeffrey Amherst carried the title of governor and collected the salary, as a reward for military services, but was not required to live in Virginia. This arrangement was a not uncommon practice. The governor's palace has been restored in Williamsburg today.

[13] Superior courts with the same jurisdiction. Literally, the terms mean "to hear and determine."

many other useful crops. From the high duty on that commodity its value is fallen, and many people are going upon hemp, which it is hoped may succeed if the bounty is continued.

This province was the first settled of any on the continent; it has always been a loyal one. The first settlers were many of them younger brothers of good families in England who for different motives chose to quit home in search of better fortune; their descendants, who possess the greatest land properties in the province, have intermarried and have had always a much greater connection with and dependence on the mother country than any other province, the nature of their situation being such from the commodiousness and number of navigable rivers and creeks that they may export to and import from home everything they raise or want from within a few miles of their own houses and cheaper than any neighboring province could supply them. They have almost always lived in good harmony with their governors and with one another; they each live at their own seats and are seldom at Williamsburg but when the public business requires their attendance, or that their own private affairs call them there. Scarce any of the topping[14] people have [a] house there of their own, but in the country they live on their estates handsomely and plentifully, raising all they require and depending for nothing on the market.

[14]Topmost in rank.

Money is at present a scarce commodity. All goes
to England, and I am much at a loss to find out how
they will find specie to pay the duties last imposed
on them by the Parliament. I have had an opportunity to see a good deal of the country and many
of the first people in the province, and I must say
they far exceed in good sense, affability, and ease any
set of men I have yet fallen in with, either in the
West Indies or on the Continent. This in some degree
may be owing to their being most of them educated
at home, but cannot be altogether the cause, since
there are amongst them many gentlemen, and
almost all the ladies, who have never been out of
their own province and yet are as sensible, con-
versable, and accomplished people as one would
wish to meet with.

Upon the whole, was [it] the case to live in America, this province in point of company and climate
would be my choice in preference to any I have yet
seen. The country in general is more cleared of
wood, the houses are larger, better, and more commodious than those to the southward, their breed of
horses extremely good and in particular those they
run in their carriages, which are mostly from
thoroughbred horses and country mares. They all
drive six horses and travel generally from 8 to 9
miles an hour, going frequently 60 miles to dinner.
You may conclude from this their roads are extremely
good. They live in such good agreement that the
ferries, which would retard in another country,

rather accelerate their meeting here, for they assist one another and all strangers with their equipages[15] in so easy and kind a manner as must deeply touch a person of any feeling and convince them that in this country hospitality is everywhere practiced.

Their provision of every kind is good; their rivers supply them with a variety of fish, particularly crabs and oysters; their pastures afford them excellent beef and mutton; and their woods are stocked with venison, game, and hogs. Poultry is as good as in South Carolina, and their Madeira wine excellent, almost in every house; punch and small beer brewed from molasses is also in use, but their cider far exceeds any cider I ever tasted at home. It is genuine and unadulterated and will keep good to the age of twelve years and more.

The women make excellent wives and are in general great breeders. It is much the fashion to marry young and what is remarkable in a stay I have made of near a month in the province, I have not heard of one unhappy couple.

The numbers of inhabitants in Virginia are supposed to be not fewer than 444,000, of near equal proportions of whites and blacks. The mulatoes are much less frequently met with here than in the more southern latitudes, and their slaves in general are more handsome and better clothed than any I [have] seen elsewhere. The generality of those born in the

[15] Carriages complete with horses and possibly a small retinue.

province are brought young to church and christ-
ened, and most parishes have one, two or three very
decent churches in them, built of brick and sashed,
in which established clergymen of the Church of
England officiate alternately.

Norfolk is the port of most traffic in Virginia. It
contains above 400 houses, has depth of water for a
forty-gun ship or more, and conveniences of every
kind for heaving down and fitting out large vessels,
also a very fine rope walk. There is a passage boat
from Hampton to Norfolk, but the pleasantest situation [from] one of them I ever saw was York, on
the beautiful river of that name, which commands a
full view of the river down towards the Bay of Chesapeake, and a pretty land view across to Gloucester
town and country, which contains some of the best
lowlands in the province. The timber resembles that
in the southern province, but I apprehend there are
none of the great magnolias northwards of Carolina.

Tulip trees are in great quantities; some I saw
not less than twenty feet round and ninety high. The
dogwood flourishes here and is covered with beautiful white flowers in April. The woods are full of a
more beautiful kind of honeysuckle than ours, but
not near so fragrant. In the back country there are
mines of lead and iron, which if properly wrought
and duly encouraged from home would turn out well.
All manner of European fruits, roots, and garden
stuff do well here, and many of the productions of
warmer countries; although oranges cannot stand

the nipping frosts and cold land winds that blow during the winter months. Their springs are uncertain and weather very changeable, which produces in spring and fall fevers and agues, which the natives themselves are very liable to. In general, I think it a more healthy country than South Carolina, and in every respect a more pleasant one.

Mr. [Francis] Fauquier was lieutenant governor in 1765 when I was there, and Sir Jeffrey Amherst Governor; the salary from home £2000 sterling and their perquisites not much less, perhaps £1500—a very good house and garden in Williamsburg.

The quantity of tobacco exported at an average of ten years past from Virginia is supposed to be from fifty to sixty thousand hogsheads annually, at about a thousand neat pounds[16] per hogshead.

About the beginning of May I crossed Potomac from Colonel Philip Lee's to Cedar Point, about 40 miles from its entrance into the Bay of Chesapeake. This river divides Maryland from Virginia and is one of the largest and most considerable in these parts, being navigable for frigates as far up as Alexandria, a place noted in this country by being that where General Braddock disembarked his unfortunate little army. The land on both banks of this river is in general good and strong, producing tobacco and most sorts of European grain. I observed scarce any pines on it, and the timber I did see began to decrease both in size and number, owing to the

16 Net pounds.

more ancient occupancy of Virginia and Maryland. The country from Potomac to Annapolis, the capital of Maryland, is extremely pleasant and very open for America; it is a light black mould which with good husbandry would last forever. It is as uneven as many counties in England and better wooded than most of them, tolerably watered, but not so much so as Virginia, nor are the people in general so opulent, although the public are in better circumstances, their paper credit being all sunk and a balance at home in their favor.

Lord Baltimore is proprietor of all this very delightful province, but has never visited it. The Roman Catholic religion is tolerated here, and its professors are very numerous and some of them in very easy circumstances.

Annapolis is charmingly situated on a peninsula falling different ways to the water which nearly surrounds it. The town is built in an irregular form, the streets generally running diagonally and ending on the town-house, others on a house which was built for a governor in Governor [Thomas] Bladen's time [the 1740's] but never finished: the plan of this was an excellent one, and the situation of it most elegant, standing on an agreeable rising ground in a beautiful lawn commanding the view of the town, the River Severn, the Bay, and all the creeks running into it. Nothing could be better chosen nor better executed as far as they went, but upon some unhappy difference between the Governor and the province the whole was stopped, the timbers and roof though ready never closed and shingled, and from the weather and moisture is now become so much damaged as never again to be in a condition to be repaired or finished.[17]

The State House and House of Council and Assembly stands also on a little hill in the town, but it as well as the church, the public school, and their other public works are going fast to decay. The present Governor, Horatio Sharpe, Esq. has a house in town, but resides much at a little place he is now building at about 6 or 7 miles up Severn River, which here falls into Annapolis Bay, forming the peninsula on which the town stands. The views all round this place are agreeable and uncommonly romantic— the banks all bluff, and such intersections and doublings of wood and water as form the most pleasant and variegated landscape. . . .

The principal staple of Maryland is tobacco and Indian corn. They are beginning to have meadows and hay. Their number of whites are wonderfully increased and said to be towards 60,000. The country in general is more healthy than those to the southward, and the gentlemen of fortune are polite and hospitable, and their women counted handsome. They are inclosed by Virginia, which makes them backward in contributing anything to the public exigencies in times of danger and difficulty.[18] I

[17]The house was finished later for St. John's College.

[18]Since Virginia protected Maryland and the latter had almost no western frontier, it felt no danger from Indians and hence no concern for defense.

cannot but lament the government's being proprietary, seeing such great and insurmountable difficulties do daily result from it.

[Upper] Marlboro is a pretty little country village situated on a creek and having a great deal of open land round it capable of much improvement. London town stands on the west side of South River, is also a pleasant village, about four miles short [southwest] of Annapolis. I am told the back country is still more pleasant and fruitful, but time did not admit of my seeing it. The face of the country much resembles Europe in general.

From Annapolis you cross Chesapeake Bay to Kent Island, about 12 miles. This island is flat and fruitful, as is the remaining part of Maryland we traversed. The channel between Kent Island and the Main to the eastward of it is narrow, and the country is very pleasant all the way to Chester, or New-town-on-Chester [now Chestertown] which though small is well inhabited. About halfway or rather more from Chester to Newcastle-on-Delaware runs the boundary line dividing Maryland from Pennsylvania. This has been long [a] matter of litigation and is not yet finally adjusted, though I was informed the commissioners are now engaged in bringing it to an issue. Newcastle is pleasantly situated, but has no trade. The men-of-war generally winter there, the river being narrow at that place, and commands the passage up to Philadelphia. It is the capital of the four associated counties annexed to Pennsylvania, but which have an Assembly and laws of their own, which in many particulars differ both with their neighbors in Pennsylvania and Maryland.[19]

The country from this town to the great and noble city of Philadelphia is extremely pleasant, well inhabited, fruitful, and full of orchards. You cross Christina [by] a ferry over a river running into [the] Delaware, which is deep and safe riding in all weathers to Chester; from that to Schuylkill ferry, between which river and [the] Delaware the city stands. The country is charming, the ferry boats are the most convenient and best served of any I ever saw; you may drive in your carriage and sit without getting out or unharnessing one horse, which is a great saving of time to travelers.

The city of Philadelphia is perhaps one of the wonders of the world, if you consider its size, the number of inhabitants, the regularity of its streets, their great breadth and length, their cutting one another all at right angles, their spacious public and private buildings, quays and docks, the magnificence and diversity of places of worship (for here all religions who profess the name of Christ are tolerated equally), the plenty of provisions brought to market, and the industry of all its inhabitants. One will not hesitate to call it the first town in America, but one that bids fair to rival almost any

[19] Delaware was granted to William Penn in 1682, received partial autonomy in 1703, but was ruled by the Pennsylvania governors until 1776. It consisted of three, not four, counties.

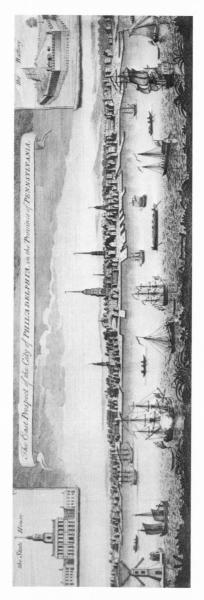

*Philadelphia, Pennsylvania*
From *The London Magazine*, October 1761

in Europe. It is not a hundred years since the first tree was cut where the city now stands, and at this time it consists of more than 3600 houses. It is daily increasing, and I doubt not in time will reach all the way from river to river, the great and far-seeing founder of it, Mr. [William] Penn having wisely laid out the space so far, which is daily taking and filling. I must not pass over two foundations here which do them much honor: their college for the education of youth, and their hospital for the reception of all sick persons whatever, including lunatics, which is supported by the benefactions of the charitable and well disposed subscribers.[20]

Doctor [William] Smith is at the head of the college, a very eminent divine. The propriety of language here surprised me much, the English tongue being spoken by all ranks in a degree of purity and perfection surpassing any but the polite part of London.

There are several large towns and villages, well inhabited and very industrious, particularly Lancaster and Bristol, but everybody of note has a residence in town, which is all built of brick and well paved, with flat foot-walks in each side [of] the streets. The Germans in this province are not under 60,000, and there are white men enough fit to bear

[20]Both the College of Philadelphia and the Pennsylvania Hospital were created through the initiative of Benjamin Franklin and his friends. He also started a subscription library, a city police, and the American Philosophical Society.

arms and able to repulse all Indians [who] could molest them, was their spirit equal to their numbers.[21] With regard to their farming you may judge when I was told they have not less than 20,000 wagons, which at four horses each would on an emergency make a body of 80,000 horse. All this province and the Jerseys bear much the face of Europe, and I have no manner of doubt, whenever Providence shall think it fit to enable America to stand alone, that Philadelphia, from its central situation and other very obvious reasons, must become the metropolis of it.

The Quakers here bear the great sway in government, which is clogged and encumbered, and I cannot help wishing that this and every other proprietary government in America was reannexed to the Crown and governed by royal governors, whose salaries ought to be permanent and independent of the fickle will and fancy of those they are sent to superintend. Till this most desirable end shall take place, America will never cordially unite or be induced to act warmly and effectually either towards their own defense or to such other purposes as may equally tend to their own, and to the honor and advantage of Great Britain.

Everybody in Philadelphia deals more or less in trade. Here they build ships and export timber of all sorts and for all purposes; many timber frames for

[21]Gordon is here lamenting the pacifism of the numerous Quakers.

the West India planters' houses are shipped from thence, their intercourse with Jamaica and all the Leeward and Windward Caribbee Islands being very considerable. Grain, hay, biscuit, beef, pork, shingles, lumber, and malt liquor are their chief exports. They live handsomely and are all going in a degree into homespun woollens and linens, which seem to be the natural consequence of restraining that branch of trade by which alone they got specie, enabling them to make remittances for British manufacturies.

The Governor of the province is named by the proprietor Penn and approved by the King. His berth is an uneasy one, as by his instructions he has it not in his power to comply with many very unreasonable requests of his Assembly, who in return generally tack his provincial salary to some bill which they are confident he neither can nor will pass. . . .

The River Delaware divides Pennsylvania from West Jersey. I crossed it at Trenton, a pretty country place, and proceeded to Princeton, where is seated a very large and spacious college, well managed with a sensible, clever master, and apartments for more than one hundred students. It is called Jersey College, or Nassau Hall.[22] All the country from this to Brunswick, where you cross a river of that name, and so to Elizabeth town, is verdant and

[22] The College of New Jersey ultimately became Princeton University. The president at this time was the Rev. Samuel Finley.

beautiful, though not so rich as Pennsylvania. At Elizabeth town I took a boat and landed at New York, about 16 miles.

I took a ride up the River Passaic from Elizabeth town for 22 miles, and in my life I never saw a more beautiful country; its banks are all clear and houses at every 500 yards on both sides of it. The falls of this river are remarkable; the whole falls into a cleft, which seems as if formed by some earthquake, near 70 feet high, soon after which it turns a mill and has over it a pretty long wooden bridge, becoming in a few miles lower navigable for small craft quite to the Bay. At the mouth of this and dividing it from Hackensack River rises a remarkable high hill, covered with wood, called Snake Hill, and all along the west side of Passaic are an infinity of salt hay meadows, which turn to good account as manure or fodder to the poor. They carry it many miles, spread it over their grass grounds as litter, or as dung, and often plough it in, after which it brings good grain and white clover in quantities. It is remarkable it will not fatten either cattle or horses, but it will keep them well up, in the state they are in, when it is first given them. 'Tis here of an inestimable value for dung and other uses, and conveyed both by land and water many miles.

This channel [now Arthur Kill] divides [the] Jerseys from Staten Island and runs up as far as Perth Amboy, the principal town of East Jersey, as Burlington on [the] Delaware, over against Bristol, is of

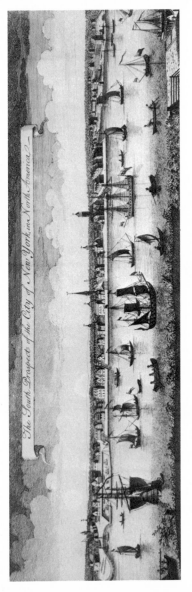

*New York City*

From *The London Magazine*, August 1761

West Jersey. I could not find there was anything very material to be seen at either of these towns, where Assemblies and courts are held alternately, and their Governor frequently has a residence at each place.[23]

The Jerseys in general are a pleasant, open, and well cultivated country, producing grain, grass, and cider in abundance. It is often called the Garden of America, and its appearance very much resembles England. The soil is not rich, but is kindly, and it is counted extremely healthful. The North, or Hudson's, River divides it from New York government till it meets the New York line, 20 miles above that point at Corbett's Point. . . .

New York Province was originally peopled by Hollanders, but was given up to Britain about one hundred years since, from which period it has enjoyed uninterrupted peace and happiness.[24] At present two-thirds of the inhabitants, as well in the province as in the town, are descended of the Dutch and Germans, who have flocked over to this and the adjacent Province of Pennsylvania in incredible numbers and make many of them excellent settlers, particularly the Germans, who can live upon less and are more industrious than any Britons.

The city of New York has long been held at home the first in America, though it neither comes up to

[23] The Governor of both Jersies was William Franklin, son of Benjamin Franklin.

[24] Hardly true. New York suffered through four colonial wars between 1689 and 1760.

Philadelphia in beauty, regularity, size, or the number of its inhabitants and houses. Of the last there are under 3000 at this time, about 300 stores, 12 churches and places of worship, and perhaps 20,000 inhabitants. Here are more Negroes than in any northern province, and by being the seat of government, civil and military, and the place to which all the money for the exigencies of America is sent from Britain, is rich. The situation of it is cool, being on a point formed by Hudson's River, which runs up many miles and is navigable above Albany, and by East River or Sound, which dividing the main from Long Island runs towards Boston and Rhode Island and forms an inland navigation safe and very commodious for many miles. Over against the town to the eastward lies a part of Long Island, which has been long peopled; the soil of it is naturally light and sandy and almost worn out, yet the old inhabitants are loath to quit this hold, on account of its remarkable healthiness and pleasantness. . . .

The land in the neighborhood of York is naturally as bad as can be and as full of stones, but the great demand for all stock and necessaries, as well for themselves as the shipping, renders it worth-while to improve all that is within reach of the town, or within reach of the banks of either of the two rivers on which it stands.

The Fort [George] is not strong; one platform mounts a great many heavy cannon. The Governor's house and garden are within the fort and are handsome and convenient.[25] The streets are not regular or wide, but standing on a descent on three sides are washed by every rain, which makes it clean and wholesome. People here live to a good old age, and very comfortably did they choose to be contented. It is hoped they will soon come to better temper, after taxes become more familiar to them.

Albany by water is [150] miles up Hudson's River, and is perhaps the pleasantest soil in the world. Their sloops are excellent and built on purpose for that trade, never going to sea. About halfway, or not quite so much, the river runs through a high ridge of mountains which they call the Highlands. Nothing can more delight an European traveller, as it differs so much in grandeur and natural magnificence from any scene he is acquainted with. The rocky steep hills are all covered with wood to the summit, and in some places the water falls over them beautifully. After you pass these Narrows, the scene grows more cultivated, and all the way up at small distances you meet settlements on each hand, mostly Dutch and German. This river has many islands and headlands, and although in the map its course appears very straight, yet the turns and breaks in it are infinite and vary the scene most agreeably at every two or three miles distance. Stones for building and limestone everywhere abound. At a little distance back from the river the

[25]The Lieutenant Governor of New York was Cadwallader Colden.

soil grows deeper, and the settlements are more numerous. At a place called Esopus, they breed the best draught and saddle horses, and all along its course the people live plentifully and pleasantly. . . . There is an old stone fort at Albany and a stockade, also a large hospital, barracks, and storehouses for a considerable number of men, but being built of wood and in a hurry, they are like every other public work in America going fast to ruin.

The people of Albany are mostly descended of low Dutch and carry down with them the true and characteristic marks of their native country, viz. an unwearied attention to their own personal and particular interests, and an abhorrence to all superior powers. I have been told it was necessary in 1765 to send a captain's command there to prevent the entire and total destruction of all the buildings and stores belonging to the King, which was but too well effected before their arrival.

In the last war it was a place of consequence, the rendezvous and headquarters from whence all orders were issued and expeditions fitted out, as well against Canada as against the French on the Lakes, to all of which places it lies convenient by means of the water communication of Hudson's River and the Mohawk River leading to Fort Stanwix. The town itself is dull and ill-built, having the gable end of their houses all to the streets, which are very dirty and crooked and confined by the rising grounds, close behind the town.

The land along the banks of the river is excellent and well improved. One Mr. Philip Schuyler has a good house near it, lately built in a better style than I have generally seen in America.[26] The family of Van Rensselaer has possession of this tract for many miles. The first view you have of Schenectady, the Mohawk River, and the country on its banks is remarkably pleasing after traveling so far over a waste. The streets of Schenectady are spacious, the river is there very beautiful, and the soil excellent. The land here and all the way up the Mohawk River is planted and sells very high. From this to Fort Johnson, up the said river, is 18 miles; it is a narrow vale or strath of excellent soil, hemmed in on both sides with high grounds, uncultivated and covered with a variety of timber, but exceedingly pleasant to the eye and cut by a thousand little brooks descending rapidly from above. It much resembles Westmoreland, or the banks of Tay above Perth.

From this, off the river about 14 miles back, Sir William Johnson has made a new settlement and has built himself a very comfortable house having a good garden and field all cleared in an absolute forest.[27] . . . He is generally crowded with Indians, mostly of the Five Nations, who are generally our friends when properly used. These are the Mohawks, Oneidas, Onondagas, Cayugas, and Senecas. These

[26] This is the house in which Anne MacVicar played. See narrative 6.

[27] Johnson's house still stands in Johnstown, N.Y., and is a historical property owned by the state and open to the public.

last are counted the bravest and most enterprising tribe of all the northern Indians; they claim an immense tract of country and exact subordination and respect through fear from almost all their neighboring tribes. They are not the best affected to the British and are so treacherous as to require a constant attention over them. I passed some days at Sir William Johnson's, but no consideration should tempt me to lead his life. I suppose custom may in some degree have reconciled him to it, but I know no other man equal to so disagreeable duty. . . .

The Fort of Niagara, which was built by the French and taken by us in 1759 by Sir William Johnson,[28] is situated on a point of land formed by the junction of the river bearing its name and Lake Ontario. From the bank of the river to the bank of the Lake runs a pretty regular work, consisting of tenaille, a ravelin, two lunettes, a bad ditch, a covered way, and a good glacis;[29] the stockade is totally gone and rotten, having been constructed in a hurry and with perishable materials, and the defenses towards the water are ill laid out of earth and sod. . . .

When I consider the very particular importance

[28] Fort Niagara was captured on July 25, 1759, after a siege by British regulars under Brigadier John Prideaux and Iroquois Indians under Johnson. After Prideaux was killed in an accident, Johnson received the surrender. It is maintained today as a historic site.

[29] A tenaille was an outwork of a fort, in the ditch between two bastions. A ravelin was a V-shaped salient with two embankments, detached from a fort. A lunette was a field work of two faces forming an angle. A glacis was the slope running down from a fort wall.

*The Horse-shoe Falls of Niagara as drawn by Isaac Weld
and engraved in 1798 for his book,
"Travels Through the States of North America,"
London, 1799.*

of Niagara from its commanding the chain of communication by water from St. Lawrence and from
New York to all the back Indian Country, I am
surprised government does not more seriously
attend to it and put it in a respectable situation. By
this navigation all our upper settlements on the
Lakes to the Illinois and even to the Mississippi may
and must be supplied; a very thorough communication and trade with all the western Indians may
be maintained and improved, and our superiority on
the Lakes established without risk or doubt, and
yet it is neglected! . . . .

About 13 miles above Niagara are the famous falls,
which are almost as difficult to describe as to represent their heighth. The breadth and quantity of
waterfall over a rock 134 feet high astonish and please
you; they greatly more than answered any idea I
had formed of them, and I doubt much if in any
part of the known world there is anything of the
kind so magnificently stupendous.

The river where it falls is about 600 feet broad,
but the constant stream occasioned by the fall pre-
vents your clearly descrying the immense height.
The water for several miles below is too strong to be
navigated, even by small boats, and for a little way
above it is not safe from the suction and rifts and
rapids. It divides its stream a little above the falls,
forming an island of small extent which but just
separates the great and smaller falls; this even would
appear great and tremendous in any other place,

except when you see them both together. I often visited these falls in June 1765 and every time I beheld them with more astonishment and satisfaction.

About two little miles above the falls we have a very neat little stockaded post on the shore called Little Niagara. Here the vessels from Lake Erie, etc. disembark their goods, which are put into wagons, or wains, drawn each by four oxen and so conveyed over the carrying place about eight miles down to the lower landing, where we have another post to protect and cover the batteaux, which at this place take on board the goods and are carried down the stream to the Fort of Niagara and so over the Lake to the River St. Lawrence, etc. . . . .

[Lord Gordon left Niagara on July 5 by ship, crossed Lake Ontario, and voyaged down the St. Lawrence.]

The Canadians are a robust, hardy, clean-made set of people accustomed from their tenderest years to cold and fatigue. They resemble greatly their Indian neighbors as well in looks and complexion as in their manners and laziness. It is true the country is good and the climate most healthful; a working man by laboring hard one day may well support himself and his family for a week, which together with some natural inconveniences may in a degree excuse their want of industry. They have generally six or seven months of frost and snow, during which time their ground can produce but little or nothing. As soon as these are past, they plough and sow and in

less than four months their harvest begins and is all
got into their barns. Their stock must all be stall fed
and are sometimes obliged to be housed all winter.
They grow about Montreal excellent wheat, corn,
barley, peas, and all manner of kitchen stuff in
abundance. I do not think the water of the river so
good as in Lake Ontario, although they have springs
and pump water enough.

Montreal, originally Ville St. Marie, stands on an
island of its name, which may be about [eleven]
leagues long and three broad. There is plenty of
meadow pasture all round it, and within a little distance, perhaps two miles, is a hill from whence you
have a very beautiful and extensive prospect of the
river, the islands in it, and all the adjoining country.
The face of it is much like a good part of Europe
and less wooded than most parts of inhabited America. The town may have about 600 houses, the
streets are narrow, it runs along the river, and is
three times as long as it is broad. There are also
three nunneries in it and several churches. The best
built part of it was burnt down in May 1765: upwards of a 100 houses in a few hours were destroyed,
and had not the wind, which was very high, most
providentially come about, the whole city might
have shared the same fate. The military were of
infinite use on the occasion. The people have never
had the precaution to have one fire engine, although
they have suffered three different times in less than
a hundred years.

Most of the noblesse of Canada have residences here, and although Quebec has been, and must always be, the key of Canada and the seat of government, yet from its situation and communication by water with all the back countries and Lakes, Montreal must always be a place of consequence, though not a place of strength. There is a good stone and lime wall with some embrasures and loop-holes all round it, which is quite sufficient to protect it from Indian insults and attacks. The house of the Jesuits will make at a very moderate expense an excellent barrack to contain twelve or fourteen companies, which number ought always to be there and is sufficient.

The whole Island of Montreal and other lands dispersed in the Province of Canada hold [that is, are held by] and belong to the Communauté de St. Sulpice in Old France and bring them an income not under £4000 sterling per year.

The women here affect dress very much and resemble in their manners, conversation, and behavior those of their mother country. Such as style themselves noblesse scarce hold any correspondence but with one another, despising all the others and calling them *des bourgeois*. They are in general rather pretty than handsome, very clever and entertaining, but not mindful of their family matters, to which they have not been accustomed, and therefore as well as on account of their religion, to which they are exceedingly bigoted, they never can make good wives for English officers, although the experiment

*Quebec, Canada*
From *The Royal Magazine*, November 1759

has been lately tried, and they seem to have no objection to such connections. The people in general and even the most sensible of them are prodigiously fond of their ancient manner of government and have not yet found out the advantages attending a free inquest by juries. Time only can open their eyes in this matter and many others, where the scale will always appear to a cool and sensible man to be of our side.

The rivers supply them well with fish, and their markets have butchers' meat good in its kind and in season. I am told that in December they lay in their stock for winter, consisting of meat and poultry and fish; these are laid in a cellar to freeze and keep good with ease and without putrefaction till the end of April or middle of May, when the frost subsides and spring recommences.

Of the French inhabitants and officers, several who had gone home on the conquest of Canada by the English[30] are returned to it; others have sold their properties to British subjects, and all have taken the oaths of allegiance and will, I think, in the succeeding generation become useful subjects, both in peace and war, if properly moulded by those who by their superior station and good example may take the lead in a point of so much essential consequence to Great Britain and America. . . .

About the end of July 1765 I left Montreal to go to Quebec by water. The passage is 60 leagues, and the country on each side the river for the greatest

[30]Canada was surrendered to the British under Gen. Amherst on Sept. 8, 1760.

part of the way is very much inhabited, having a parish church at the distance of every eight or nine miles; many times they are placed opposite to one another and have a very agreeable effect.

The channel of this river is in many places narrow and difficult, yet capable with good pilotage to admit twenty-gun ships as high almost as Montreal. The country from Montreal to the plains of Maskinonge is all cultivated, but these being liable to be overflowed in the springs and falls are used only as hay meadows; they are of a considerable extent and interspersed with woods, creeks, and marshes. However, the hay is excellent and in great quantities most years; they house it all in barns built on the spot and elevated above the high flood mark, and they convey it to their habitations either up or down the river in summer in boats, in winter on sleds (a kind of vehicle everywhere used in Canada during the seven winter months). They are drawn generally by one horse, and in them the ladies and gentlemen go a visiting both in town and country during the continuance of the snow; they travel 60 miles a day over rivers, lakes, and morasses and through woods which for the rest of the year are totally inaccessible. They are both open and covered, and when they are made large to hold four people in them, like the body of a coach, they put more horses to them, according to the weight to be drawn. In this season everything of heavy carriage is transported, as timber, stone, iron ore, grain, etc.

The banks of the St. Lawrence are more thickly

inhabited than of any river I ever saw, and I am told while it was in possession of France they could by signal and communication of cannon from parish to parish, and by flags and signals which every captain of militia had at his door on a long pole, like a May pole, convey an alarm all the way from Montreal to Quebec in a very short time, an advantage attending their method of settling which in our provinces were never thought of.[31] . . .

Just at Quebec the River St. Lawrence is more narrow than anywhere from Frontenac to its mouth, being not more than 1100 yards over, and from this it was our batteries demolished all the Lower Town, the Chateau St. Louis, the cathedral, the bishop's house, and almost every good house, in even the Upper Town.

This famous city is situated on a commanding point of land formed by the influx of the River St. Charles into that of St. Lawrence. The highest part of the Upper Town, called Cape Diamond, commands all round and with a good citadel, which it undoubtedly ought to have, would be immensely strong. There is a vacant space betwixt that and the town which shelves down towards the Lower Town, at the back of which the rock in most places is almost perpendicular and very high. On the edge of this

[31] Gordon is referring to the French "ribbon" farms, which fronted on a river narrowly, being a few hundred feet wide, and then ran back inland two or three miles. While less convenient to cultivate than a square, this design permitted the houses to be fairly close together along the river bank.

precipice, hanging over the Lower Town, stands the King's house, called Chateau St. Louis. No situation can be better chosen or more grand, for it commands the view of the basin, which is capable of containing any fleet, the Lower Town, and the road before it towards the River St. Lawrence where ships come to an anchor, besides all the Côte de Lauzon, the Point Levis, the Isle of Orleans, and part of the banks of Montmorency. It is much demolished, as are the cathedral and Episcopal palace, which stands a little lower, yet has almost as commanding a prospect. In good policy these buildings should all be repaired, as is already almost every house in the Lower Town and many in the Upper.

The Jesuits have here a noble college, built round a square, and a good garden; it would make an exceeding good barrack for a regiment, including officers. The Recollets have also a house and garden, as have the seminary for the education of youth, which is large and spacious and is now refitting. Their garden is one of the best, and their establishment must ever be useful. There are two convents for women in town, and another very large establishment called the General Hospital for sick and wounded of both sexes, which is about a mile and a half out of town on the River St. Charles, has a good deal of land in property, and will always be serviceable. These ladies paid great attention to our sick and wounded officers and soldiers and deserve the royal protection.

The country on every side of Quebec is strong and well worth seeing for a soldier. The works are badly constructed and may be enfiladed[32] from beyond the River St. Charles; they would require a numerous army to defend them and an open communication with the sea. It always has [been] and always must be the key to Canada, which now seems to be a natural part of our American empire and ever should have been thought so, nor should we upon any account ever part with it. . . .

Quebec in time of peace is well supplied with all provisions, fish and flesh, and is I think one of the most agreeable quarters in America. Indeed, I would prefer Canada for society and conversation to any province I have yet seen; the people are good humored, sensible, very polite, and fond of strangers; they are gay and not giddy, and brave without boasting of being so; their women in general know a good deal and are both handsome and agreeable. Upon the whole, when one thinks of an hundred thousand souls in Canada, all of whom must now be supplied from Great Britain, a large extent of country the best of which is still to [be] peopled and cultivated, and these a hardy race, born to arms and to fatigue, I for one must always esteem Canada a most essential acquisition to America and not less so to Britain, provided she is sensible enough to see and improve the advantages which this colony may be of to both. . . .

[32] Shot upon from, in this case with favorable results for the attacker.

[Lord Gordon returned to Montreal in August, then went up the Richelieu River to Lake Champlain, a part of New York he had missed before.]

On both sides of Lake Champlain the land is but middling, as well as on the islands, some of which are large and well wooded. Crown Point is finely situated on a promontory running out into the lake, the River au Sud going to Ticonderoga bounding it on one side, and the Bay on the other. The fort is of wood, built in a most masterly manner. It has five bastions, mounts 105 guns, and has casemates for 4000 men, and to hold provisions *de guerre et de bouche*[33] for four months. It has cost much money and trouble, and as the wood work is beginning to give, if it is not taken in time it will in a year or two more be in as bad a state as the other American forts I have seen. It becomes less an object since Canada is ours, but must always command these lakes. Scarce any guns are mounted, the ditch is all cut or blown in a limestone rock, but is not finished, nor the glacis, nor is any outwork of any sort except three fortified redoubts with cannon. . . .

Ticonderoga stands on an eminence on the point formed by the river from Lake George which at this place falls into Lake Champlain. The works are ruinous. It is a quarré all of wood, and some bad casemates; it is much commanded by the high ground behind it, along which from the river to the lake Mons. de Montcalm constructed his famous

[33] That is, ammunition and food.

lines which we attacked unsuccessfully in 1758:[34]
they are a short mile distant from the fort, were
immensely strong, having three or four batteries
all five-logs high and as well laid out for defense as
the nature of the ground could admit it. . . . At
some small distance from the fort nearer the lake,
we have a fortified redoubt which commands the
harbor, where all the lake vessels are laid up in winter and some of them have been built. . . .

[After inspecting the several forts between Lake
Champlain and the Hudson, Lord Gordon passed
through Albany again on his way into western
Massachusetts.]

Four miles farther you cross a very steep and high
hill, after which you have a tolerably good road to
[Great] Barrington, a pretty scattering country village situated amongst rocks and [Berkshire] hills
covered with brush and pines. From this through
Sheffield to Canaan [Connecticut] you pass through
a delightful vale well planted and thickly inhabited,
with orchards to every house, which are here warm
and well built, the men well clad, and the women
remarkably tidy and handsome. From Canaan to
Norfolk the country is romantic and young peopled,
the roads are middling, being not above twenty years
settled. From this you travel 14 miles through the
green woods, the worst road I have seen in America.
This is a new cut and not a habitation all the way,

[34] This is the attack Chaplain John Cleaveland witnessed,
in narrative 4.

though I am told there will soon be several. After you pass this forest of noble chestnuts and other trees, but no oaks, you fall in on a pretty little river[35] at a place called New Hartford, which you descend all the way to Simsbury, a pleasant little village twenty miles short of Hartford, the capital of Connecticut. All this country is fully settled and is just like England.

Hartford is a large scattering town on a small river which, as well as that at Simsbury, falls into Connecticut River. It has two handsome meeting [houses] on a platform of their own; the people are uncommonly stiff and formal and as industrious as in any one province. Here they build vessels for the lumber trade to the West Indies, from 100 to 150 tons, and float them down in freshets in spring and fall. The number of inhabitants in Connecticut are supposed about 100,000, and their militia roll about 30,000, that is from 16 to 60 years of age. All the country to Enfield through Windsor is fully inhabited, and all along the Connecticut River, up and down, fine rich meadows and fields. . . .

To Worcester the soil and views continue most striking and agreeable. This is one of the best built and prettiest inland towns I remember to have seen in America. It is fine land all the way to Shrewsbury, and good road; from this all the way to Boston it is populous and pleasant. The best road is to quit the Post road three miles east of Shrewsbury and fall again into it a mile west of Weston.

[35] Farmington River.

*Governor Thomas Pownall's view of Boston,
about 1758*

From the Clements Library

On this road you meet with houses and villages all the way to Boston, which stands on a peninsula with a narrow neck or causeway, which is the only access by land to it. It has been settled about an hundred years, 1616[36]— next to Virginia—has in it 2100 houses, many of which are better, more spacious, and more commodious than those I saw either at Philadelphia or New York. They all have gardens, and within it is a Common and a Mall, and two remarkable rising grounds called the Beacon Hill and the Fort Hill. From these you command all the town, the harbor, the Castle, the River Charles, and all the country, and I doubt much if there is in the world a finer or more variegated prospect. The Main Street is two miles long, leading from the gate all the way to the ferry which plies over Charles River to Charleston, a very pretty village rather older than Boston and very well served.

The number of inhabitants in town are supposed to be about 23,000; in the Province of Massachusetts, 350,000, and about 10,000 fit to bear arms, but this calculation is rather high. This is more like an English old town than any in America. The language and manner of the people very much resemble the old country, and all the neighboring lands and villages carry with them the same idea. The better kind of people in and near the town seem well bred and sensible. They lament their present plan

[36] Gordon is wrong. Boston was settled in 1630, which was 135 years before his visit.

of government, which throws too much weight into the popular scale; they know by experience the bad consequences attending that circumstance. When the Stamp Duty was first laid by act of Parliament in 1765, the first and most flagrant acts of opposition to it and of riotous and licentious spirit in the mob broke out here and were fatal to the house and property of their Lieutenant Governor, Mr. Hutchinson.[37] . . .

The entrance of Boston Harbor is nine miles off. It has but one considerable channel for large ships, and that is in many places crooked and very narrow. About three miles below the town stands Castle William on an island. It is a very small quarré without works much exceeding the fort. Shirley's battery of forty-pounders might damage any ships considerably before they could bring their broadsides to bear, but otherwise it is not strong. I am told sixty-gun ships have been quite up to the town, and some say there are five fathoms in the worst of the channel, which may be totally blocked up by sinking one vessel across it. The harbor is full of islands, bays, and shoals: there is on one island almost opposite to the fort, called Shirley Island, a church and small town, and a blockhouse and battery on another. The fort might mount 140 guns, the barracks there might

---

[37] A mob ransacked and robbed Gov. Thomas Hutchinson's splendid house on the night of Aug. 26, 1765. Although he opposed the Stamp Act, he supported the right of Parliament to tax the colonies.

contain a thousand or twelve hundred men. On the whole, what is there is in better repair and more completely furnished than any provincial fortification I have yet seen in America.

Although the face of the country is very rough and stony about Boston and some miles round, yet it is a most healthy climate and kindly soil, producing every European grain and root in plenty and perfection, besides Indian corn. I never saw such quantities of apple and pear trees; all the roads are lined with them. The poorest farmer or rather proprietor has one or more orchards, and cider is their common drink, although they grow good barley and hops grow there, everywhere, with little trouble or culture, more large and high than any I remember in Surrey. Cider is so plenty as to sell at a dollar a barrel, cask included—34 gallons.

The men here resemble much the people of Old England, from whence most of them are sprung. I was rather surprised to find here, and not amongst the richest, the respectable names of Howard, Wentworth, Pelham, Pierpoint, Dudley, Carey, Russell, Temple, and many others of less note and ambiguity; but the levelling principle here everywhere operates strongly and takes the lead. Everybody has property and everybody knows it.

The women here, and at Rhode Island, are accounted the most beautiful of any on the continent, and I am apt to believe it is so. At a ball of seventy ladies I saw about one-half handsome ones; perhaps one reason is that every girl who has a pretty face and good clothes is free to come and is well received at public places there, where there is no sort of distinction of persons.

The country from Boston to Providence, 45 miles, is mostly rough and stony, but there is a fine plain near Providence called Seekonk-Plain, and a beautiful river called Pawtucket, on the west side of which and within a mile is a spermacetti work for candles, which cost about one shilling and sixpence per pound. Providence is a large town built on the banks of the river and having several good houses in it. Here and at Newport they hold their general courts for Rhode Island, which is the smallest province in America, containing about 40,000 whites and 5000 Negroes. The harbor of Newport is good and deep enough for any ships to come in.

From Newport to [New] York is a good navigation through the Sound, about 200 miles. The Narrows toward York is very pleasant till you come to a place called Hell Gate, where you must have a pilot and choose your time or tide, else it is not to be risked. Near this and a little lower is Morrisania,[38] the seat of Lewis Morris, Esq. and the prettiest and best conditioned farm in America. It is nine miles

[38] Tha manor of Morrisania, located in what is now the Bronx, had been purchased by Lewis Morris's grandfather in 1670. The present occupant managed the large estate and inherited it in 1762. He was a signer of the Declaration of Independence. His house was burned by the British army during the Revolution, but was rebuilt.

from York, consists of 2050 acres, for which he has been offered £22,000 sterling. It has a bad house on it.

From York harbor to Sandy Hook is about ten leagues, after you pass the Narrows, which are formed by two points of Long Island and Staten Island. You meet with sand banks which render it necessary to take in a pilot; he generally leaves you about the lighthouse on Sandy Hook, after which you have no stop but Nantucket shoals, about 25 leagues off and bearing from the Hook east half southerly. Behind the Hook when at sea, you make the highland of Neversink, which in very clear weather is seen at least 10 leagues off and appears at first like an island. On sounding all hereabouts one may catch good sea bass and black fish in plenty, with ground bait.

I embarked at New York on the 14th of October 1765, on board the Harriet packet, Captain Robin son, for Falmouth.

# Index

# INDEX

List of The Lakeside Classics

# The Lakeside Classics